100% EMPLOYEE ENGAGEMENT— <u>GUARANTEED</u>!

A Three Step Formula for Getting More Done, Having More Fun and Generating Way More Profit

Ross Reck, PhD
Tracy Myers, CMD
Thom Scott

Published by Ross Reck Publishing
P. O. Box 26264
Tempe, AZ 85285-6264
602-391-3250
www.rossreck.com

Printed in the United States of America

10 9 8 7 6 5 4 3 2 1

ISBN-10: 0-9852346-2-8

ISBN-13: 978-0-9852346-2-1

INTRODUCTION

Before we get started, our first order of business is to provide you with an example of what employee engagement looks and feels like. This way we'll all be of the same frame of mind as we journey through this book. The example involves Xerox Corporation and we found it in a book titled *Business Adventures* by John Brooks which was originally published in 1969 and reprinted in 2014.[1]

On September 16, 1959, Xerox (then called Haloid Xerox) revolutionized the copying industry by introducing the Xerox 914 copier. It was the first commercially successful plain paper copier and it went on to become the top-selling industrial product of all time.[2] There was so much interest in this product that its first public demonstration was shown on live television in New York.[3]

By early 1960, the time had come to mass produce the 914. The production facility was an old loft building located on Orchard Street in Rochester, New York. Horace W. Becker was the Xerox engineer who was primarily responsible for bringing the 914 from the working-model stage to the production line.[4] Mr. Becker describes the scene when the employees on this project became engaged with their work: "It was at Orchard Street that we finally caught fire. Don't ask me how it happened. We decided it was time to set up an assembly line, and we did. Everybody was keyed up. The union people temporarily forgot their grievances, and the bosses forgot their performance ratings. You couldn't tell an engineer from an assembler in that place. No one could stay away—you'd sneak in on a Sunday, when the assembly line was shut down, and there would be somebody adjusting something or just puttering around and admiring our work."[5] As this example illustrates, there's a certain magic that occurs when employees become engaged with their work—they're excited, willing to cooperate and work hard, and everyone is emotionally connected to each other and to their work.

The purpose of this book is to show you how to create this same exciting magic in your organization. It presents a *new* leadership model that *guarantees* full employee engagement. If you implement this model in your organization, 100 percent of your employees will become engaged with their work—all working at their full potential just as they did in the Xerox example. This should be exciting news to all business leaders especially since a recent global study conducted by the Gallup organization found that only 13 percent of employees are engaged with their work.[6] This means that slightly more than one in ten employees are willing to do whatever it takes to make their company successful. On the other hand, nearly nine in ten aren't working anywhere near their potential— they're either apathetic toward their job, doing the minimum amount to get by or actively doing things to undermine the success of the business.

In 1960, Douglas McGregor laid a solid foundation for tapping into this unutilized potential in his book, *The Human Side of Enterprise*. Keep in mind, the term "employee engagement" was not in common usage at the time, but McGregor was fully aware of the low level of employee engagement that existed even then. As he put it, "Many managers would agree that the effectiveness of their organizations would be at least doubled if they could discover how to tap into the unrealized potential present in their human resources."[7] He reasoned that the traditional management model, which he referred to as *management by direction and control*, denies individuals the opportunity to satisfy certain needs at work that are important to them. As a result, using this management model actually *prevents* businesses from tapping in to the full potential of their employees.[8]

McGregor concluded that a new methodology based on new thinking was necessary if businesses were going to succeed in tapping into this unutilized potential. He knew the effect he wanted to achieve; he called it the *Principle of Integration* (today we call it employee engagement)—creating a set of conditions where employees can achieve their own goals *best* by directing their efforts to the success of the organization.[9] In other words, the harder employees work for the success of the business, the more satisfaction they experience regarding their personal needs.

The purpose of this book is to pick up where McGregor left off and finish the job—to present a completely new methodology based on new thinking, which makes it not only possible, but easy for the leaders of a business to tap into the full potential of their employees. This methodology points out exactly what needs to be done in order to create an environment where employees can achieve their own goals *best* by directing their efforts to the success of the organization. As a result, instead of having only 13 percent of your employees engaged with their work, you'll have 100 percent of them engaged—all working up to their full potential. Think of what this can mean to the success of any business organization—profit or nonprofit.

This book is divided into five parts. The first presents the employee engagement problem which is the fact that the global level of employee engagement is only 13 percent. Chapter 1 then demonstrates how understanding human motivation is the key to solving this employee engagement problem.

The second part of this book presents the cause of the employee engagement problem which is that businesses insist on clinging to a management model that actually *prevents* employees from becoming engaged with their work—it's called the Traditional Management Model. Chapter 2 illustrates how the Traditional Management Model works and shows why it prevents employees from becoming engaged with their work.

Part Three presents the solution to the employee engagement problem which is: businesses need to switch to a new model that *causes* employees to become engaged with their work. Chapter 3 tracks the creation of such a model which is called the Engagement Formula and shows how it causes employees to become engaged with their work.

Part Four presents case studies of six highly successful companies whose leadership practices embrace the Engagement Formula. Four of these are large companies that range from 10,000 employees to nearly 50,000. These are W. L. Gore & Associates, Google, SAS and Southwest Airlines. One is a medium size company which is on-line shoe and apparel retailer Zappos which has 1,400 employees. There is also one small company, Frank Myers Auto Maxx, which is a used car dealership that has 35 employees.

The final part of this book presents a detailed Implementation Planning Guide for implementing the Engagement Formula in your organization.

Unlike most books written in this genre, *100% Employee Engagement—<u>Guaranteed!</u>* doesn't over-promise and then under-deliver. Rather, it delivers exactly what it promises—a new leadership model that guarantees an employee engagement level of 100%.

DEDICATION

To the memory of Douglas McGregor, Abraham H. Maslow, Frederick Herzberg and Wilbert L. Gore: the pioneering thinkers who laid the groundwork for this book.

ACKNOWLEDGEMENT

Were it not for the patience, kindness, encouragement, support, willingness to proof-read on demand and the insightful suggestions of Marcia Reck, this book would never have been written.

TABLE OF CONTENTS

PART ONE – THE EMPLOYEE ENGAGEMENT PROBLEM:

BUSINESSES ARE EXPERIENCING VERY LOW LEVELS OF EMPLOYEE ENGAGEMENT—WORLD-WIDE

CHAPTER 1

UNDERSTANDING HUMAN MOTIVATION IS THE KEY TO SOLVING THE EMPLOYEE ENGAGEMENT PROBLEM

The leadership of any business would love to have a high level of employee engagement for a number of very good reasons that we're all familiar with. First, employee engagement is the primary driver of profitability, productivity, innovation, employee loyalty, customer loyalty and stock price. Second, companies with a high level of employee engagement outperform companies with a low level of employee engagement, enjoy substantial cost savings due to reduced employee turnover, absenteeism, accidents and theft, and they are magnets for attracting the best talent. Clearly, having a high level of employee engagement is *the* way to operate a business.

As it turns out, employees would also love to have a high level engagement. It's not something you have to force them to do. They're dying to become engaged with their work. The reason is that when employees are engaged with their work, they have an emotional attachment to it—their work has become part of who they are. As a result they come to work each day excited about giving every bit of energy, creativity and passion to performing their job. Life as an employee doesn't get any better than this.

So, here we have a situation where both the leadership of a business organization and its employees benefit in a big way from a high level of employee engagement. This being the case, one has to ask the question: "Why is the global level of employee engagement only 13 percent?" Why isn't it closer to 100 percent? If both the leadership of a business and its employees want a high level of employee engagement and it's not happening on a large scale, something is preventing it from occurring. The question is what?

Before we can answer this question, we first need to figure out one very basic, but critical piece of information about employee engagement and that is: *what is it?* Right now, we really don't know. Yes, we do have many definitions of employee engagement, but they all describe what it looks like, not what's actually going on. We don't know from a cause and effect standpoint exactly what employee engagement is. Once we know what it is, it will be obvious what's preventing it from occurring on a large scale. So, the first order of business is to figure out exactly what employee engagement is and we're going to do that in the remaining part of this chapter.

EMPLOYEE ENGAGEMENT IS ALL ABOUT MOTIVATION

The fact that some employees are engaged with their work while the vast majority of others aren't tells us that employee engagement is all about all one thing— *motivation*. This brings up the age old question of what really motivates us. In reality, the answer is quite simple. It's something called *self-interest*—pursuing the satisfaction of needs that are important to us. Every single one of us comes into the world already programmed to pursue the satisfaction of a set of inborn needs. This how we're genetically wired—it's part of our DNA. From birth to death, our behavior is completely defined by our pursuing the satisfaction of those needs.

Keys to Understanding Human Motivation

Since we're all motivated to pursue the satisfaction of a set of inborn needs, it's important that we understand what those needs are and how they work. (It should be noted that all parenthetical statements contained in the rest of this chapter are those of the authors.)

Human Beings Are Perpetually Wanting Animals

As soon as one need is satisfied another appears in its place. This process is unending and continues from birth to death. As Douglas McGregor put it, "Man continuously puts forth effort—works, if you will—to satisfy his needs."[1]

A Satisfied Need is Not a Motivator of Behavior

When you're hungry, all you can think of is food. Once your stomach is full, food no longer motivates you. As Abraham Maslow put it, "If we are interested in what *actually* motivates us, and not what has, will or might motivate us, then a satisfied need is not a motivator. It must be considered for all practical purposes simply not to exist, to have disappeared."[2] In other words, people are only motivated by *unsatisfied* needs.

Human Needs are Organized in a Hierarchy of Importance

The most well known depiction of this hierarchy is that presented by Abraham Maslow.[3] We know you're all familiar with the Maslow need Hierarchy. In fact, some of you are probably thinking, "Oh no! Not this again." But please bear with us because the Maslow need hierarchy holds the key to explaining why the global level of employee engagement is so low. With this in mind, let's take a fresh look at Maslow's hierarchy.

THE MASLOW NEED HIERARCHY

An Illustration of the Maslow need hierarchy is presented below:

At the lowest or most basic level in this hierarchy are our physiological needs. These are the requirements for our survival—food, water, air, etc. When these needs are fairly well satisfied, the needs at the next level, which are our safety needs, emerge and take over our behavior. In turn, when the needs at this level become fairly well satisfied, the needs at the next level emerge and so on. It's important to note that before the needs at the next level can emerge and take over our behavior, the needs at *all prior levels* must be fairly well satisfied. We will now reexamine each of Maslow's five need levels and how it relates to employee engagement.

Physiological Needs

Providing for the satisfaction of employees' physiological needs is fairly easy for a business organization to accomplish. All it has to do is provide an adequate pay check along with reasonable benefits and employees have the means to satisfy their physiological needs and keep them satisfied. However, providing for the satisfaction of employees' physiological needs, by itself, is not sufficient to engage them with their work. At the same time, if these needs are not well satisfied, this will actually prevent employees from becoming engaged with their work. The reason is that unsatisfied physiological needs create distractions for employees which means they cannot give their full attention and effort to performing their jobs. For example, if employees aren't making enough money to support themselves, they will worry and fret over how they're going to make ends meet. This is why companies with a high level of employee engagement such as SAS, JetBlue, Google, NetApp and Southwest Airlines make it a point to provide their employees with compensation that is at or above their industry average along with a benefit package that's fairly generous. They want to minimize these distractions so employees can focus on performing their jobs. As stated on the SAS web site, "They (employees) should be freed from many of the distractions of day-to-day life, so they can focus on doing their best work."[4] Similarly, Eric Schmidt, Executive Chairman of Google had this to say when discussing Google's philosophy regarding employee benefits. "The goal is to strip away everything that gets in our employees' way (of doing their best work). We provide a standard package of fringe benefits, but on top of that are first-class dining facilities, gyms, laundry rooms, massage rooms, haircuts, carwashes, dry cleaning, commuting buses—just about anything a hardworking employee might want. Let's face it: programmers want to program, they don't want to do their laundry. So we make it easy for them to do both."[5]

Safety Needs

When our physiological needs become fairly well satisfied, the needs at the next level emerge and begin to dominate our behavior. These are our safety needs—safety from harm, safety from accidents, personal security and job security. Providing for the satisfaction of employees' safety needs is also fairly easy for a business to accomplish. All it has to do is provide a reasonably secure job and a workplace that's relatively pleasant and safe and these needs are satisfied. As is the case with physiological needs, providing for the satisfaction of employees' safety needs, by itself, is not sufficient to engage them with their work. At the same time, if these needs are not well satisfied, this will actually prevent employees from becoming engaged with their work. The reason is that unsatisfied safety needs also create distractions for employees which means they cannot give their full attention and effort to performing their jobs. For example, if employees are concerned about being laid off, they will be spending time and energy thinking about and looking for a new job which takes time and energy away from their performance on their current job. This is why companies with a high level of employee engagement such as W. L. Gore & Associates and Southwest Airlines make it a point to provide their employees with a pleasant work environment and a secure job. They want to minimize these distractions so employees can focus on their jobs. Bill Gore, founder of W. L. Gore & Associates understood very well that you can't engage your associates (employees) when they're not feeling safe and secure.[6] For this reason, Southwest Airlines has a firm "no layoff" policy. The company has not laid off a single employee since the beginning of the company.[7]

Social Needs

Once our physiological and safety needs are fairly well satisfied, our social needs emerge and take over our behavior. Social needs include the need for friendship, to belong, to be accepted by others and to be part of a family. Maslow, however, left one very important item off of his list of social needs—although it's strongly implied—that's fundamental to explaining the low level of employee engagement. It's the need to be treated as an *equal*. The ultimate form of acceptance to any group is to be accepted as an equal. Anything less is simply not acceptance.

Equality is critical because it means autonomy—the freedom to question, the freedom to challenge and the freedom be yourself, have fun, and do your job as you see fit. At Google, which was recently ranked by *Fast Company* as the most innovative company in the world, equality is its innovative edge. There, everyone is committed to finding the best idea. The leaders at Google understand that this process often involves lots lively debate among fellow employees with strongly held differing opinions. These kinds of discussions can only take place when no one has veto power—everyone has to be equal.

Providing for the satisfaction of employees' need to be treated as an equal is not as easy as it is for their physiological and safety needs. A business organization can't just write a check and be done with it. Instead, the leaders of that business have to become actively involved with the rest of the employees and set the example when it comes to treating everyone as equals. This is why companies with high levels of employee engagement like W. L. Gore & Associates, SC Johnson and Google refer to their employees as "associates," "family members" or "fellow Googlers." It's to reinforce the fact that everyone who works there is equal and therefore has the autonomy to do their job as they see fit. As former Google CEO Eric Schmidt said in an interview while discussing the Google culture, "No particular person has a strong say....At Google, everyone is the same." He then shared an anecdote to illustrate this point. During his first year as CEO, he was in a meeting with the founders of the company and the other senior executives. Mr. Schmidt wanted to hire one of his friends to work at Google, but he couldn't convince anyone else at the meeting that this person should be hired. As a result, the hiring did not take place. After the meeting, he was venting his frustration over the fact that he couldn't hire his friend when one of the early founders of the company came up to him and said, "Don't feel bad Eric, I can't get any of my people hired either." His comment following the anecdote was, "I thought to myself, this is the ultimate statement that at Google, everyone is the same."[8]

Esteem Needs

When our physiological and safety needs as well as our need to be treated as an equal are fairly well satisfied, our esteem needs surface and take over our behavior. According to Maslow, all of us have a strong desire for a high evaluation of ourselves. Furthermore, this high evaluation must be authentic—based on real capacity, real achievement, and real respect from others.[9] What this means is that unlike the satisfaction of physiological, safety and social needs, satisfaction of our esteem needs is not something that the leadership of a business can give us—it's something we have to *earn* through our actions. And the only way we can earn it at work it is through the experience of exercising our autonomy over the performance of our jobs—deciding what to do, how to do it and then doing it. This is why most people strongly resent it when their boss micromanages them. It denies them the opportunity to exercise their autonomy in ways that lead to the satisfaction of their esteem needs.

Satisfaction of our esteem needs results in feelings of self-respect, self-confidence, achievement and self-worth. Experiencing satisfaction of our esteem needs is what makes us feel really good about ourselves. Therefore, if the leadership of a business wants to tap into this powerful source of motivation, what it needs to do is provide employees with the opportunity to exercise their autonomy over the performance of their jobs. This is why companies with a high level of employee engagement operate from a leadership philosophy of, "give people the tools they need to do their job and then get out of their way."[10] Leaders at these companies do not go around giving orders to other employees. Rather, their role is to provide support, remove obstacles and barriers and do whatever else it takes to enable fellow employees to do their job in an excellent manner. As one employee at W. L. Gore & Associates put it, "If you tell anybody what to do here, they'll never work for you again."[11]

While providing the opportunity for employees to exercise autonomy over their work taps into a very powerful source of motivation, it's still not enough to engage employees with their work. One more thing is still necessary before employee engagement can occur. With that in mind, let's look at the remaining level in the Maslow need hierarchy.

The Need for Self-Actualization

When the first four levels of the Maslow need hierarchy are fairly well satisfied, our need for self-actualization emerges and takes over our behavior. The need for self-actualization is the need to find meaning in our lives. According to Maslow, even when all the previous need levels have been fairly well satisfied, people will still have a craving for something more unless they are doing something they feel is *worthwhile*.[12]

At work, people want more than just a job; they want to be part of something special. They want to make a contribution to something that matters where they feel they can make a difference and know that their life stands for something good. Worthwhile work then, provides an individual the opportunity to satisfy their need for meaning. Maslow had this to say about the importance of worthwhile work: "The more I think about it, the more difficult I find it to *conceive* of feeling proud of myself, self-loving and self-respecting, if I were working for example, in some chewing gum factory, or a phony advertising agency, or in some factory that turned out shoddy furniture. I've written so far of 'real achievement' as a basis for solid self-esteem, but I guess this is too general and needs more spelling out. Real achievement means inevitably a worthy and virtuous task. To do some idiotic job well is not real achievement. I like my phrasing, 'What is not worth doing is not worth doing well.'"[13]

For example, Ross was doing some consulting for a large and reputable manufacturer of agricultural equipment. This manufacturer had just acquired a company that manufactured lawn and garden equipment. Ross was speaking with an engineer who worked for this newly acquired company. His job was to design a new weed whacker (a hand-held piece of equipment powered with a gasoline engine that cuts down weeds). He said that when he attended engineering school he was taught to design the best possible equipment he could. He also said that his company wanted him to design a weed whacker that would last for only 50 hours of use. The idea was that at some point shortly after 50 hours of use, the machine would break down thereby requiring the customer to buy a new one. He said that he could easily design the machine to last 500 hours or more at almost no extra cost but his company told him to design one that would last only 50 hours. His comment was, "My company is asking me to design junk. I didn't become an engineer to design junk—designing junk makes me feel bad. Therefore, I'm looking for a job with another company." Here we have a case of an engineer who was experiencing the satisfaction of all of the first four levels of the Maslow need hierarchy—he was paid well with great benefits, a secure job and had all the autonomy in the world to exercise over the performance of his job. But since he was being asked to design junk, he did not feel that his job was worthwhile—it did not satisfy his need for meaning. As a result, he was not able to become engaged with his work.

Now here's where things start to become interesting. When work holds meaning for the individual doing it, it begins to assimilate into the identity of that individual. According to Maslow, "...work actually becomes part of the self, part of the individual's definition of himself."[14] This is why employees at organizations with a high level of employee engagement often refer to their company with the term "we" as in, "We're building a new facility in New York" or, "We're getting ready to introduce a new product line" as if the company is something they own—they have assimilated their work into their personal identity. <u>When this occurs, this is when employees become engaged with their work</u>. This means that *self-actualization and employee engagement are the same thing*!

Bingo! Now we know exactly what employee engagement is and when it occurs. It's called *self-actualization* and it occurs the instant employees are able to satisfy their need for meaning through performing their job. We also know exactly what is necessary before employee engagement can occur. An organization must provide its employees with the opportunity to experience the satisfaction of *all five levels of the Maslow need hierarchy*. (It should be noted that Frederick Herzberg in 1959[15] and Douglas McGregor in 1960[16] essentially reached the same conclusion.)

At this point the question becomes, "Don't different people have different ideas of what they consider to be worthwhile work?" The answer is obviously yes. This is why companies with a high level of employee engagement place a very strong emphasis on the process by which they hire new employees. As will be pointed out later in this book, they go to great pains to make sure they hire only those people who are going to find meaning in performing the kind of work being done at their particular company. In order for self-actualization to occur there must be a tight fit between what an individual sees as being worthwhile work and the work opportunities being offered by an organization. Maslow described this fit as being, "...like a key and a lock.... There is an interaction, a mutual suitability, like a good marriage or like a good friendship, like being designed for each other."[17]

Maslow also concluded that self-actualization at work plays an important role in our happiness. As he put it, "This business of self-actualization via a commitment to an important job and to worthwhile work could be said, then, to be the path to human happiness....The only happy people I know are the ones who are working well at something they consider important."[18] This is why employees who are engaged with their work appear to be so happy—it's because they are happy! As one employee at Zappos put it, "Happiness! WOW, what a concept.... I started this job as just that, a job. Zappos has become my passion...a passion that is present in my encounters with strangers, my interactions with family and friends and in my personal well being. I can, without a doubt, say that I am happy because of the passion I have for my life at Zappos."[19]

CONCLUSIONS ABOUT HUMAN MOTIVATION

It's *Impossible* to Motivate People at Work

Why? Because they're *already* motivated—to pursue their self-interest. The only thing the leadership of a business can do if it wants its employees to perform at a high level is to *engage* the motivation that's already there—to create a situation where the harder people work toward pursuing the satisfaction of their own needs, the harder they work toward the goals of the organization. This all important behavioral fact did not escape the attention of Douglas McGregor. In his book, *The Professional Manager*, which was published posthumously in 1967, he wrote, "The answer to the question managers often ask of behavioral scientists...—How do you motivate people?—is: You don't. Man is by nature motivated....We do not motivate him because he *is* motivated. When he is not, he is dead."[20]

Companies with a high level of employee engagement understand this. Instead of trying to motivate their employees with traditional means like authority, rewards and punishment, they've created environments where employees are free to be themselves, have fun and follow their passion (the motivation that's already there inside them). This is why the underlying managerial philosophy at SAS is, "Give people the tools they need to do their job and then get out of their way."[21] At W. L. Gore & Associates, there are no titles, no orders and no bosses. Associates (the Gore term for employees) identify an area where they think they can make their best contribution and then they are encouraged and supported to maximize their accomplishments. As company founder Bill Gore once said, "We don't manage people here, they manage themselves."[22]

Self-Actualization and Employee Engagement are the Same Thing

Employee engagement occurs when employees are able to experience the satisfaction of all five levels in the Maslow need hierarchy. This means that if the first four levels of the Maslow need hierarchy are fairly well satisfied and employees do not feel the work they are doing is worthwhile, then employee engagement cannot occur. For example, a friend of ours took a job as a production supervisor for a company that made a variety of corn and potato chips. At first he absolutely loved his job—he was well paid, the job was very secure and he was able to exercise lots of autonomy over the performance of his job—he couldn't wait to get to work in the morning. Several years later, we heard that he had quit working for that company. When we asked why, he said, "All of the fun went out of the job the day I realized that the company didn't make one thing that was good for people." In other words, he no longer felt the work he was doing was worthwhile and, as a result, became disengaged from it. Maslow's quote bears repeating here: "What is not worth doing is not worth doing well."

People want to be Engaged with Their Work

When employees work in an environment where they are free of most day to day distractions, are treated as equals and provided with the opportunity to exercise their autonomy doing work that they feel is worthwhile, they feel very, very good about themselves and what they're doing. In fact, life as an employee doesn't get any better than that. This is why companies with a high level of employee engagement experience employee turnover rates that are far below their industry average—people absolutely love working there. Here's what one employee had to say about working at Zappos: "Zappos culture is unlike any other! Going to 'work' is fun, enjoyable, yet productive! I leave work tired; often dirty, but fulfilled and happy—an odd combo, hey? It's a relief to walk around and see your work family laughing, playing and SMILING, all while doing their job of WOWing customers! That's what Zappos is all about. We are encouraged to work hard, play hard and I love it!"[23] An employee at NetApp said it this way, "I've been given lots of freedom to implement my ideas to make things better and also am able to make decisions in order to get the job done. At the end of the day I can look back and see what I have been able to accomplish with a great feeling of satisfaction."[24] This being the case, we can conclude that employees very much *want* to be engaged with their work—it's not something you have to force them to do; they're dying to become engaged with their work.

Therefore, if employees *want* to be engaged with their work and they're not, something is *preventing* that from happening. The next step in our journey is to figure out what that is.

PART TWO - THE CAUSE OF THE EMPLOYEE ENGAGEMENT PROBLEM:

BUSINESSES INSIST ON CLINGING TO A MANAGEMENT MODEL THAT *PREVENTS* EMPLOYEES FROM BECOMING ENGAGED WITH THEIR WORK

CHAPTER 2

THE TRADITIONAL MANAGEMENT MODEL AND WHY IT PREVENTS EMPLOYEES FROM BECOMING ENGAGED WITH THEIR WORK

The Traditional Management Model assumes that people have an inherent dislike for work and if left on their own, they will do very little. In other words, people are lazy and it's management's job to motivate them.[1] (This is interesting in light of the fact that we just concluded that it's impossible to motivate people at work.) Below is a brief description of how the Traditional Management Model works:

Step One: <u>Management</u> decides upon and communicates the performance expectations to employees.

For example, the administrator of a hospital might require each department to achieve a certain average score each month on the surveys patients fill out regarding their satisfaction with their stay at the hospital. Or, a CEO may require each of his or her company's business units to achieve a certain level of profitability each quarter.

Step Two: <u>Management</u> monitors the performance to see how it compares to expectations.

Step Three: <u>Management</u> provides feedback on performance supported by rewards and punishment.

If actual performance meets or exceeds the performance objective, management is happy and rewards, tangible or otherwise, may be forthcoming to the individuals responsible. If actual performance falls short of expectations, feedback on how to improve performance will be provided along with some possible negative consequences such as a less than stellar performance review. If actual performance continues to fall short of expectations, the negative consequences may be more severe. As Douglas McGregor put it, the implicit logic is "...that in order to get people to direct their efforts toward organizational objectives, management must tell them what to do, judge how well they have done, and reward or punish them accordingly."[2]

WHY THE TRADITIONAL MANAGEMENT MODEL PREVENTS EMPLOYEES FROM BECOMING ENGAGED WITH THEIR WORK

We've just learned that employees become engaged with their work when they are able to experience satisfaction of all five levels of the Maslow need hierarchy. <u>If _any_ of the five need levels are not satisfied, then employee engagement cannot occur.</u>

The problem with the Traditional Management Model is that it places managers in a position of dominance over the people they are managing. Managers are the authority figures or bosses while the employees who report to them are referred to as their "subordinates." The problem with this superior/subordinate relationship is that it denies employees the opportunity to satisfy their need to be treated as equals. Without equality, employees do not have the autonomy that's necessary to pursue satisfaction of their esteem needs which is the next level in the Maslow need hierarchy. Furthermore, if employees' esteem needs go unsatisfied, pursuing the satisfaction of their need for self-actualization is not even a possibility. As a result, employee engagement cannot occur.

Conclusion: It's *Impossible* to Create a Highly Engaged Workforce Using the Traditional Management Model

What this means is that if a business insists on using the Traditional Management Model, the best it can hope for is a workforce filled with disengaged employees—people who are passive, unhappy, resentful or even rebellious. These people are not interested in doing whatever it takes to make the business successful. It follows then that organizations which insist on using the Traditional Management Model are leaving lots of money on the table and putting their very survival at serious risk. Clearly, if the goal is to create a highly engaged workforce, a new methodology for dealing with employees that's based new thinking is required. As Albert Einstein put it, "Insanity is doing the same thing over and over again and expecting different results."

WHY ARE SO MANY BUSINESSES STILL USING THE TRADITIONAL MANAGEMENT MODEL?

The reason is that many of the people in managerial and executive positions have bought in so strongly to the Traditional Management Model that they can't see beyond it. And the reason they can't see beyond it is they don't want to because they absolutely love it—*for all the wrong reasons.* First, the Traditional Management Model is the only management model they know. It's what they learned in school, what they observed their mentors using and what the overwhelming majority of businesses throughout the world are organized around. So they're very comfortable with it. Second, the Traditional Management Model elevates the status of managers over the rest of the employees. Along with this elevated status come perks and privileges that are not available to the rest of the employees. All of this makes managers and executives feel like they are part of a privileged class. Third, the Traditional Management Model makes it possible for managers and executives to do their job without having to interact with their subordinates all that much. All they need to do is look at their computer and monitor performance numbers—there's no need for them to get their hands dirty. This further reinforces the notion of belonging to a privileged class. Finally, the Traditional Management Model makes managers and executives feel like they're in complete control—they set the performance standards, monitor actual performance and administer rewards and punishment. And, if performance happens to fall short of expectations, they have a built in scapegoat; they can blame their subordinates. After all, the managers have done their job—they communicated the performance standards to their subordinates and provided them with feedback based upon their performance. Therefore, if their subordinates underperform, it can't be the manager's fault; it's because the subordinates themselves are lazy, stupid or uncooperative. As far as most managers and executives are concerned, what's there not to like about the Traditional Management Model? It's easy to see why so many refuse to let go of it.

On the other hand, the reality is that the Traditional Management Model prevents employees from becoming engaged with their work which causes organizations that use it to severely underachieve.

PART THREE - THE SOLUTION TO THE EMPLOYEE ENGAGEMENT PROBLEM:

BUSINESSES NEED TO SWITCH TO A NEW MODEL THAT *CAUSES* EMPLOYEES TO BECOME ENGAGED WITH THEIR WORK

CHAPTER 3

CREATING A NEW MODEL THAT CAUSES EMPLOYEES TO BECOME ENGAGED WITH THEIR WORK

If we're going to abandon the Traditional Management Model, the question then becomes, "What do we replace it with?" Since no real alternative exists at this time, we're going to have to create one. While this may initially seem like a difficult challenge, it's actually pretty straightforward. From the prior discussion on human motivation, we already know that *employee engagement and self-actualization are the same thing.* This means that employee engagement occurs when employees are able to experience the satisfaction of *all five levels of the Maslow need hierarchy.*

For example, let's take a look at a company that really knows how to engage its employees—Southwest Airlines. Southwest has made a profit every year since 1973 in an industry where a number of its competitors suffered multi-billion dollar losses. In addition, its workforce is the most loyal and productive in the industry and the airline is consistently rated at or near the top when it comes to customer service. In order to gain an understanding of how Southwest is able to do this, let's take a brief look at its culture.

1. Southwest takes excellent care of its employees

At Southwest, the pay is at or above industry average and the benefits are excellent including a company sponsored

401(k) plan, profit sharing, stock purchase plan and an affordable health package.[1] Also, Southwest provides a fun and pleasant work environment with a very high level of job security—it has never laid off any of its employees.[2] This means that the physiological and safety needs of Southwest's employees are fairly well met.

2.   *At Southwest, all employees are treated as "family members."*

This means that every employee, regardless of title, is treated as an *equal*—no one is more important than anyone else and everyone is treated with the utmost dignity and respect. For example, the pilots help the flight attendants pick up the trash in the plane during quick turnarounds.[3]

3.   *At Southwest, employees are encouraged to be themselves and have fun.*

This means that employees are encouraged to exercise their *autonomy* by being themselves, having fun and do their job as they see fit. They have the freedom to make decisions and are encouraged to think outside the lines.[4] For Example, on some flights a flight attendant may sing the safety briefing or deliver it in rap rather than just speaking it. This results in many more passengers actually listening to it.

4.   *Southwest employees are proud of their company and strongly believe in what it stands for.*

This provides Southwest employees the opportunity to satisfy their need for *meaning* through their work—knowing they are working for a worthy cause.[5]

What Southwest has succeeded in doing is creating a workplace where employees are able to experience <u>*the*</u>

satisfaction of all five levels of the Maslow need hierarchy which, in turn, engages them with their work. Now, all we have to do is to figure out a way to duplicate what Southwest Airlines is doing and we're home free. This brings us to the Engagement Formula.

THE ENGAGEMENT FORMULA

It's important to note that the Engagement Formula is not referred to as a new *management* model. Rather, it's referred to as a new *leadership* model and the choice of words is important. The term *management* implies top down control in an environment where nearly everyone is a subordinate. As was pointed out earlier, this prevents employees from becoming engaged with their work. Leadership, on the other hand, implies that employees are free to exercise autonomy over the performance of their jobs in an environment where everyone is an equal. Below is a description of what the Engagement Formula is and how it works.

Step One: Create a Full-Engagement Culture that Defines the Organization and Drives Performance

A full-engagement culture has four basic elements:

- **Minimal Distractions—So Employees Can Focus on Performing Their Jobs**

- **Single Status—Everyone is an Equal**

- **Mission—This is What We Do**

- **Core Values—This is How We Do It**

Each of these four elements will be discussed below.

Minimal Distractions—So Employees Can Focus on Performing Their Jobs

As was pointed out earlier, unsatisfied physiological and safety needs create distractions for employees which means they cannot give their full attention and effort to doing their best work. This is why companies with a high level of employee engagement such as Southwest Airlines, Google, W. L. Gore & Associates and S. C. Johnson offer compensation packages that are at or above industry levels, provide fairly generous benefits, a job that is reasonably secure and a work environment that's pleasant and safe. They want to remove as many distractions as possible so their employees can focus on performing their jobs. For example, SAS, which has been listed on the *FORTUNE* "100 Best Companies to Work For" for 16 straight years,[6] offers competitive compensation and has been recognized for its generous benefits package. In addition, SAS is second to none in terms of workplace amenities and the jobs are very secure—the company has never laid off a single employee. The goal is to reduce stress and distraction so employees can focus on doing their best work.[7]

Single Status—Everyone is an Equal

A single status culture means everyone within that culture is an equal and has the same level of influence. This means that all symbols of *unequal status or privilege* must be removed—things like separate parking lots, separate dining rooms, time clocks for some employees and not others, special parking spaces for "important people" and so forth. This doesn't mean there can't be different job levels and pay levels within an organization. What it does mean is that differences in job levels and pay levels cannot signify or suggest that someone is superior, better or more important than someone else. Also, any "us vs. them" attitudes must be replaced with a "we're all in this together" attitude. There's no room for arrogance in a single status culture. In addition, information must be shared with everyone at once rather than going to the "important" people first and eventually filtering down to the less important people.

As was mentioned earlier, this is why companies with high levels of employee engagement like W. L. Gore & Associates, Southwest Airlines, DreamWorks and Google refer to their employees as "associates," "family members," "DreamWorkers" or "Googlers." It's to reinforce the fact that everyone who works there is equal and therefore has the autonomy to do their job as they see fit. SAS clearly gets the equality message across by not differentiating benefits between employees. Service workers (such as housekeepers) have the same choice of health plans, child care services, health care and fitness programs as the CEO. In addition, all SAS employees are paid on a salaried basis.[8] The only people paid by the hour are substitutes and students. Google also has a single status culture. According to the Google web site, "At lunchtime, almost everyone eats in the office café, sitting at whatever table has an opening and enjoying conversations with Googlers from different teams. Our commitment to innovation depends on everyone being comfortable sharing ideas and opinions. Every employee is a hands-on contributor, and everyone wears several hats. Because we believe that each Googler is an equally important part of our success, no one hesitates to pose questions directly to Larry or Sergey (the founders of the company) in our weekly all-hands ('TGIF') meetings—or spike a volleyball across the net at a corporate officer."[9]

Mission—This is What We Do

A mission is a brief statement of what an organization does or stands for. For example, the mission of online apparel and shoe retailer Zappos is to "provide the best customer service possible." At W. L. Gore, the mission which has endured for more than 50 years is simply "to make money and have fun doing so." The mission of JetBlue is "bringing humanity back to air travel." A mission, by itself, may not seem all that profound, but when combined with a set of core values, these two concepts together can transform a workplace into something that's very special—something that employees believe in and are proud of.

Core Values—This is How We Do It

Core values communicate how the employees within an organization go about the business of executing its mission. For example, the mission at Zappos is to provide the best customer service possible. They have developed the following set of ten core values that define how the company will go about executing its mission:[10]

- Deliver WOW Through Service

- Embrace and Drive Change

- Create Fun and A Little Weirdness

- Be Adventurous, Creative and Open-Minded

- Pursue Growth and Learning

- Build Open and Honest Relationships With Communication

- Build a Positive Team and Family Spirit

- Do More With Less

- Be Passionate and Determined

- Be Humble

These core values represent behavioral expectations for Zappos employees and thus direct their efforts toward the goals of the organization. Zappos CEO, Tony Hsieh has this to say about core values: "It doesn't actually matter what your company's core values are. What matters is that you have them and that you commit to them. What's important is the alignment that you get from them when they become the default way of thinking for the entire organization."[11] In other words, when a set of core values is in place and everyone in the organization is committed to them, employees no longer need a boss to tell them what to do and how to do it. They already know what to do—that's the mission. They also know how to do it (execute the mission) thanks to the set of core values. Having bosses telling employees what to do and how to do it is how businesses attempt to achieve control under the Traditional Management Model. Under the Engagement Formula, control is achieved through a mission and a set of core values that *everyone* is committed to.

For example, "Deliver WOW Through Service," tells employees that simply pleasing the customer is not enough. Zappos employees are expected to blow the customers' socks off. This means continually coming up with new and innovative ways of doing so. "Create Fun and A Little Weirdness" tells employees that they are free to be themselves and have fun while doing their jobs even if that means being a little weird. "Be Humble" communicates clearly that arrogant, condescending and mean spirited behavior are not tolerated at Zappos. Within the context of these core values then, Zappos employees are free to exercise their autonomy to do their job as they see fit. Nobody is there to look over their shoulders.

It's also important to note the process by which Zappos came up with these ten core values. At his previous company, Tone Hsieh was fed up with all the backstabbing and ladder climbing he saw. When he joined Zappos, he was determined that things would be different. One of the first things Mr. Hsieh did was ask the company's 300 employees at the time to list the core values that the Zappos culture should be based upon. The initial list had 37 core values.[12] During the course of a year, Mr. Hsieh emailed the entire company several times to get suggestions and feedback on which core values were most important to Zappos' employees. Like-minded suggestions were then grouped together until the exercise yielded the ten core values that continue to drive the company today which now has more than 1,400 employees. According to Mr. Hsieh, "I was surprised the process took so long, but we wanted to make sure not to rush through the process because whatever core values we eventually came up with, we wanted to be ones that we could truly embrace. ...We wanted a list of committable core values that we were willing to hire and fire on. If we weren't willing to do that, then they weren't really 'values.'"[13]

Putting together a set of core values in this manner resulted in instant buy-in from the employees because they came up with them. From that point forward, only qualified prospective employees who mesh with these ten core values get hired.

Step Two: Hire Only Qualified People Who Mesh With the Culture

Companies with a high level of employee engagement are extremely *disciplined* about using their culture as the primary criterion for hiring new employees. In order for employees to become engaged with their work, there must be a tight fit between what those individuals see as being worthwhile work and the work opportunities being offered by the organization. This is why companies with a high level of employee engagement have two parts to their interview process for hiring new employees. The first is to determine whether a perspective employee is a good professional fit for the company and it looks at the usual things like technical competence, background experience, education and so forth. The second part of the interview process is to determine whether or not the person is a good fit with the culture. Technically qualified people who don't mesh with the culture simply don't get hired because they wouldn't they wouldn't be happy or productive working there. They would be what Amazon.com refers to as a "cultural misfit."[14] This is why Google hires only 0.5 percent of the people who apply for a job there; they want to make sure the cultural fit is tight because when the cultural fit is tight, people don't need to be managed, they manage themselves.

For example, Zappos, which hires approximately one out of every 100 applicants because it will only hire people who fit tightly with its culture, puts job candidates through two separate sets of interviews.[15] The hiring manager and his or her team will interview the prospective employee to determine whether or not he or she is a good professional fit for their team. They will look at usual things such as technical competence, background experience and so forth. Then the

Human Resources Department conducts a second set of interviews to determine if this person will mesh with the Zappos culture. If he or she doesn't, then no matter how professionally qualified they are, they don't get hired. According to CEO, Tony Hsieh, "They actually have questions for each and every one of the (ten) core values."[16]

Mr. Hsieh continues, "One of our values is, 'Create fun and a little weirdness.' So one of our interview questions is, literally, on a scale of 1 to 10, how weird are you? If you're a 1, you're probably a little too straight-laced for us. If you're a 10, you might be too psychotic. It's not so much the number; it's how candidates react to the question. Because our whole belief is that everyone is a little weird somehow, so it's really more just a fun way of saying that we really recognize an celebrate each person's individuality, and we want their true personalities to shine in the workplace environment, whether it's with co-workers or when talking with customers."[17]

NetApp communicates very clearly to job candidates what it will be looking for during the interview process. "We will evaluate you on your technical skill set, communication style and culture fit, not the way you dress."[18] (Please note that all parenthetical statements throughout the rest of this paragraph are those of the authors.) At Southwest Airlines, a good attitude (cultural fit) is the most important element when hiring. This is why in 2013 Southwest hired only 1,521 new employees from the 100,682 resumes it received—Southwest is looking for a tight cultural fit.[19] According to former CEO, Herb Kelleher, "We don't like to, but we will sacrifice expertise, education and experience to get a good attitude."[20] The mindset at Southwest is that if a prospective employee has the right attitude (i.e., meshes with the Southwest culture), they can teach that person what they need to know to do their job.

W. L. Gore & Associates posts this advice for prospective job seekers on its web site: "At Gore, hiring decisions—like most decisions—are made by a small team of associates. This hiring team typically includes the people who will be working with you day-to-day as well as leaders and others with specific experience in your field. This gives all of them a chance to assess whether you are a good match for Gore (cultural fit) and for the team (professionally qualified)."[21] Google is not only obsessed with the quality of its employees, it's also obsessed with how they fit into the Google culture. That's why in addition to the interview process that determines a job candidate's technical competence, there's also a "Googliness" screen to determine if he or she can fit into the Google culture.[22]

The Hiring Process Must be Supported with a Relevant Training and/or Sponsorship Program that Teaches and Reinforces the Culture

Organizations with a high level of employee engagement support their hiring process with a relevant training and/or sponsorship program that teaches and reinforces the culture. They don't expect new employees to assimilate the company's culture on their own. For example, at W. L. Gore & Associates everyone has a sponsor who is committed to helping them succeed. An important part of succeeding is learning to live and work within the Gore culture. According to the Gore web site, "Sponsors are responsible for supporting your growth, providing good feedback on your strengths and areas that offer opportunities for development and for helping you connect with others in the organization."[23]

At Zappos, once a prospective employee gets past the interview process, he or she must then go through a four-week Customer Loyalty training program. This is true for all new hires, even those at the executive level. During this program, new hires absorb and begin to live the Zappos culture. This training includes at least two weeks in the call center on the phone dealing with customers. Anyone who acts as though this type of work is beneath them is immediately shown the door.[24] Also, in order to make sure that these new hires are truly embracing the Zappos culture, at the end of each week they are offered $2,000 on top of their current week's pay if they will agree to quit the company.[25] The goal is to weed out people who are not really committed to working at Zappos.

Step Three: Leaders Must Lead, Not Give Orders

In a full-engagement organization, there is no need for leaders to tell their followers what to do and how to do it—they already know this from their organization's mission and core values. Instead the role of a leader is to set the example and do whatever it takes to enable his or her followers to do an excellent job. Examples of what leaders do in high-engagement organizations are presented below.

Leaders Set the Example

In a full-engagement culture, leaders set the example when it comes to treating everyone as equals and living the organization's core values. Herb Kelleher, former CEO of Southwest Airlines set the standard when it came to living his company's core values. It was not uncommon for him to show at an airport, after midnight, dressed in a set of coveralls and carrying a box of doughnuts to help the cleaning the crews clean planes. This sent a very clear message that just because he was the CEO, it didn't mean he was above doing the dirty work required to make an airline successful. Also, on the day before the American Thanksgiving holiday which is the busiest travel day of the year in the US, he would spend a full shift loading bags because he wanted his employees to understand that he knew, first hand, how hard is was to do their job on the busiest travel day of the year. These types of activities gained Mr. Kelleher a great deal of respect from Southwest's employees.

Leaders Provide Support

Leaders ask questions, listen and remove barriers and obstacles. In other words, their job is to do whatever it takes to enable the people around them to do an outstanding job. No job is too menial if it enables another employee to do an excellent job. For example, in addition to helping flight attendants pick up trash in the plane during quick turnarounds, the pilots at Southwest Airlines also help gate agents push wheel chair passengers on to the plane so that Southwest can make an on-time departure.

Leaders Make Sure the Culture Stays Healthy

One of the most important aspects of a leader's job is to make sure none of the negative or dysfunctional aspects of the Traditional Management Model work their way back into the culture. We're talking about things like symbols of unequal status, leaders telling their followers what to do and how to do it or some employees trying to turn their personal preferences into rules that they want everyone else to follow.

This is a high priority at W. L. Gore & Associates. According to CEO Terri Kelly, "The leader's job is to make sure the culture is healthy: Is it working as a system? Are teams coming together? Are we getting diverse points of view? Are the best ideas rising to the surface? Our leaders have to be comfortable with not being at the center of all the action, with trying to drive every decision, with not being the most strategic person on the team or the one with most thoughtful ideas. Their contribution is to help the organization scale and be effective."[26]

CEO Tony Hsieh, checks on the health of Zappos culture once a month with a *happiness survey.*[27] Employees are asked if they agree or disagree with statements like the following:[28]

- I believe that the company has a higher purpose beyond just profits.

- My role at Zappos has a real purpose – it is more than just a job.

- I feel that I am in control of my career path and that I am progressing in my personal and professional development at Zappos.

- I consider my co-workers to be like my family and friends.

- I am very happy in my job.

Results of this survey are broken down by department and opportunities for improvement are identified and acted upon.

The employees of The World Famous Pike Place Fish Market in Seattle, Washington meet once a month to assess the health of their company's culture. At each meeting, the same three questions are addressed: What's working? What isn't working? What needs to be changed?[29]

Making the Transition from Executive or Manager to being a Leader

One of the perceived obstacles associated with implementing the Engagement Formula is that managers and executives are going to have to embrace front line employees as equals which may initially be outside some of their comfort zones. Under the Traditional Management Model, managers and executives could hide behind their status or in their offices if they weren't comfortable mixing it up with front line employees. Those options are simply not available in a full-engagement culture. Under the Engagement Formula, the role of a manager is transformed into the role of a leader. Furthermore, it's the leader's job to set the example when it comes to living out the company's core values and treating everyone as an equal. This may be a new and unfamiliar role for some of them. On the other hand, experience has shown that once they commit to making the transition, they will soon embrace their new role.

As an example of leaders embracing this new role, Charles S. Jacobs, author of *Management Rewired*, shared a story from when he was a consultant for Bethlehem Steel. Throughout its history, Bethlehem Steel could have been the poster child for the Traditional Management Model. According to Jacobs, the line between workers and managers was clearly defined by the company and reinforced by the union. Each of Bethlehem's steel mills had a country club next to it that was exclusively for management. In addition, the management of the company was housed in an office building that was located well away from the gritty business of making steel. In Bethlehem, PA, management lived on one side of the city while the workers lived on the other. Also, there were different dining rooms in the headquarters building for the different levels of the hierarchy and they were furnished accordingly.

By the early 1980's, foreign competition and the mini mills changed the nature of the steel industry and integrated steel producers like Bethlehem were no longer profitable. According to Jacobs, "One by one, Bethlehem's country clubs were sold off and the mills shut down....With the business dying and nothing left to lose, many in the company were willing to turn the traditional management relationship upside down."[30] At one of the divisions, a team of supervisors was given a free hand to redesign the business with Jacobs' help. The group decided that each phase of the production process would be run by a dedicated team and all decisions would be made with the participation of those who would be impacted, including the union. As Jacobs put it, "Effectively, all supervision was done away with and people were trusted to do the right thing."[31]

Jacobs goes on to say, "The general manager and his executive staff redefined their roles to support the employees. They moved from the six-story headquarters building with closed offices, sitting outside the plant, to a one story metal building with an open bullpen in the center of the mill. For the first time in the history of the company, an all-hands meeting was held for both the union and management to discuss the changes, and information that used to be held close to the vest was shared widely, including financial results."[32]

Through lots of hard work over the next two years, the teams were able to cut $170 million in expenses. Unfortunately, it was not enough to save this particular division—it was still losing $30 million a year. When he heard the news that the division was being shut down, Jacobs drove to Bethlehem to meet with the people he had worked with on the redesign of that division. While having lunch with a supervisor who had been one of the most skeptical members of the team at the beginning of the project, Jacobs said, "...I wondered aloud if there was anything we could've done differently. He told me that we had done the best we could, and that we'd succeeded in convincing the other divisions of the company to adopt our approach. It just wasn't enough to overcome the drastic changes roiling the markets for structural steel. Then he added, *'I've been here for thirty-five years, but the last two years have been the best of my career.'*"[33] The truth is that most managerial and executive types, once they experience working within the Engagement Formula, will absolutely love their new role because of the deep sense of meaning and connection it provides.

The Payoff for Implementing the Engagement Formula in Your Organization

If you choose to create a fully engaged workforce by implementing the Engagement Formula in your organization, you'll notice some major changes emerging almost immediately. Your employees will begin to create a competitive edge for your organization that your competitors can't easily copy—your costs will be significantly lower due to greatly reduced turnover, absenteesim, theft and accidents, while your revenue dramatically goes up because your newly engaged employees are actively searching for innovative ways to improve products, services and customer experiences. Listed below are the kinds of things you can expect once you implement the Engagement Formula in your organization:

- Incredible levels of profitability, productivity, customer loyalty and employee loyalty that are enjoyed by companies like Southwest Airlines, W. L. Gore & Assiociates, JetBlue and Costco.

- Extraordinary success at delivering "WOW" customer service the way leading companies like Amazon.com, Marriott Hotels, Nordstrom, Zappos and Publix Super Markets do.

- Exceptional levels of innovation found in companies like Google, 3M, Apple and Johnson & Johnson.

- Your organization will become a magnet for attracting the best talent like Google, SAS and Southwest Airlines.

Examples of highly successful organizations whose leadership practices embrace the Engagement Formula are presented in the next section of this book.

The Engagement Formula—Summary

STEP ONE: CREATE A FULL-ENGAGEMENT CULTURE THAT DEFINES THE ORGANIZATION AND DRIVES PERFORMANCE

A full-engagement culture has four basic elements:

- **Minimal Distractions—So Employees Can Focus on Performing Their Jobs**

- **Single Status—Everyone is an Equal**

- **Mission—This is What We Do**

- **Core Values—This is How We Do It**

STEP TWO: HIRE ONLY QUALIFIED PEOPLE WHO MESH WITH THE CULTURE

- **The Hiring Process Must be Supported With a Relevant Training and/or Sponsorship Program that Teaches and Reinforces the Culture**

STEP THREE: LEADERS MUST LEAD, NOT GIVE ORDERS

- **Leaders Set the Example**

- **Leaders Provide Support**

- **Leaders Make Sure the Culture Stays Healthy**

PART FOUR - CASE STUDIES:

EXAMPLES OF HIGHLY SUCCESSFUL ORGANIZATIONS WHOSE LEADERSHIP PRACTICES EMBRACE THE ENGAGEMENT FORMULA

INTRODUCTORY NOTE

It should be noted that the founders and leaders of the following high-engagement organizations did not have the benefit of any firm guideposts like the Engagement Formula as they put their organizations together. They pretty much followed their gut instincts. They all knew what they didn't want: a Traditional Management Model type of organization that emphasized things like structure, chain of command and predetermined communication channels. At the same time, they all knew what they wanted: a workplace where employees came first—a place where they were free to create, innovate, be themselves, have fun and apply their best efforts toward the success of the organization. What's interesting is that while the founders and leaders of each of these organizations took a different journey when it came to putting their organizations together, the leadership practices they eventually came up with are pretty much identical. Without realizing it, they all followed the Engagement Formula.

W. L. GORE & ASSOCIATES

W. L. Gore & Associates is a privately-held company that was founded in 1958 by Wilbert "Bill" L. and Genevieve "Vieve" Gore. It has more than 10,000 employees located in 34 countries and sales this past year were more than $3 billion. While best known for GORE-TEX fabrics, Gore has used its proprietary technologies with the polymer polytetraflourethylene (PTFE or better known as Teflon) to create numerous innovative products for the electronics, fabrics, industrial and medical markets. Currently, Gore manufactures more than 1,000 different products.

Mr. Gore worked at DuPont as an engineer for 17 years before leaving to found W. L. Gore & Associates. While at DuPont, Mr. Gore developed a disdain for the Traditional Management Model types of organizations with their rules, hierarchies, chain of command and formal channels of communication. He often said that "communication really happens in the car pool."[1] What he meant is that in a Traditional Management Model type organization like DuPont, the car pool was the only place where employees could talk freely to each other without regard for the chain of command.

Mr. Gore also observed that during times of crisis, the formal hierarchical organization was thrown out the window and replaced with a number of small teams to deal with the critical issues and problems at hand. Team members functioned as equals—there was no hierarchy. Team members rode to work together, worked around the clock if necessary in order to get things done and rode home together—all the while talking about what needed to be done to alleviate the current crises. Mr. Gore observed that these were the times when organizations took risks and made big breakthroughs. This observation led to some breakthrough thinking on the part of Mr. Gore—*why do we have to wait for a crisis before we organize like this; why can't we create an organization where things are like this all the time.*[2]

And, that's exactly what he did when he founded W. L. Gore & Associates. He created an organization where there were no positions of status, no titles, no chain of command and no formal channels of communication. He referred to this organization as a "lattice" organization where everyone was free to communicate with everyone else without having to go through an intermediary. Since W. L. Gore & Associates is a privately held company, there is no way to determine how profitable it is. Nonetheless, it is an extremely successful organization. It has made the *Fortune* list of the Top 100 Companies To Work For 17 consecutive years and has been named one of the best workplaces in the UK, Germany, France, Sweden and Italy several years in a row. In addition, W. L. Gore & Associates was declared by *Fast Company Magazine* to be the most innovative company in America.

Let's take a look at how the leadership practices at W. L. Gore & Associates match up with the Engagement Formula.

THE ENGAGEMENT FORMULA AT W. L. GORE & ASSOCIATES

Step One: Create a Full-Engagement Culture that <u>Defines</u> the Organization and <u>Drives</u> Performance

A full-engagement culture has the following four elements:

Minimal Distractions—So Employees Can Focus on Performing Their Jobs

Unsatisfied physiological and safety needs create distractions which means employees can't give their full energy and attention to performing their jobs. This is why companies with a high level of employee engagement offer compensation packages that are at or above industry levels, provide fairly generous benefit packages, a job that is reasonably secure and a work environment that's pleasant and free from danger. They want to remove as many day to day distractions as possible so their employees can focus on doing their best work. W. L. Gore & Associates is no exception.

According to the W. L. Gore & Associates web site, the company's fundamental beliefs in fairness, the long term view and that everyone is in the same boat underlie its total compensation strategy. "We strive to be internally fair and externally competitive. Unlike companies that base an employee's pay on the evaluations of one or two people—or on supervisors' opinions alone—Gore involves many associates in the process. To ensure that everyone is paid fairly, we ask associates to rank their team members each year in order of contribution to the enterprise. In addition to the numerical ranking, we invite comment on the rationale behind the ranking, as well as on particular strengths or potential areas of improvement for the associates on the list.

Of equal importance, we ensure that our pay is competitive by taking part in an extensive benchmarking. Each year we compare the pay of Gore associates from varied functions and roles with their peers at other companies.

We are committed to long-term sustainable business growth, and believe we are 'all in the same boat' working toward that common goal. Our objective is to compensate associates based on their overall contribution to Gore."[3]

At Gore, the benefits offered reflect the company's value for its associates. According to the company's web site, "Our success is based on the capability and creativity of our associates, so our benefits offerings and design reflect our value for their contributions. Gore benefits programs are comprehensive and externally very competitive."[4]

From the company's web site, Gore's benefit programs include:[5]

- **Associate Stock Ownership Plan**: ASOP is the centerpiece of our benefit platform globally. ASOP provides associate with equity ownership in the company while building financial security for retirement. It enables all associates to have an opportunity to participate and share in the growth of the company by acquiring ownership.

- **Health and welfare**: Gore provides an array of healthcare benefits for associates globally, including medical, dental, and vision plans.

- **Income replacement**: Life insurance as well as long-term disability insurance is available for associates and their families.

- **Balancing work and family life**: Many of Gore's benefits and services help associates balance the increasing demands of work and family.

- **Professional and personal development**: Gore encourages associates to discover a path that best fits their own interests while helping the company succeed.

Although we have no hard data, it's safe to conclude that the jobs at W. L. Gore & Associates are very secure. The reason is that the founder of the company, Bill Gore, understood that the key to his company's long term success was innovation—continually developing high quality new products that were "revolutionary" in there effect rather than "me-too" products. He also understood that if people don't feel safe and secure in their jobs, they won't become engaged with their work. It follows then, if they're not engaged with their work, they're not going to innovate and there goes the success of the company. The only remotely related statistic we were able to come up with is that Gore's voluntary employee turnover rate in the US this past year was three percent[6] which, according to the Great Place to Work Institute is about one-fifth the industry average.[7] This means people love working at Gore. Also, Gore would not have made the *Fortune* list of 100 Best Places to Work for 17 consecutive years if the jobs at the company weren't extremely secure.

Gore also offers a pleasant and safe work environment that is conducive to team work and innovation. According to the Great Places to Work Institute, "Gore plants are all smoke-free, hold and abundance of natural light, contain offices of similar size (no matter who the occupant is), and house shifts of a limited number of associates (approximately 200). It's one way that associates in any one facility are encouraged to know each other and what's going on in the plant....Gore's campus-like plant settings lend themselves to recreational opportunities. The Delaware-Maryland plant cluster offers two on-site fitness centers, soccer fields, basketball courts, volleyball courts, a driving range, nature area, trails and large recreational pavilion. The Arizona cluster includes a walking trail, volleyball and basketball courts."[8]

From the above discussion, it's pretty straightforward to conclude that the physiological and safety of the Gore associates are fairly well satisfied. This means there are few, if any, day to day distractions that would keep them from giving their full energy and attention to performing their jobs.

Single Status—Everyone is an Equal

Gore is obsessed about everyone being an equal. According to the Gore web site, since day one, "...Gore has been a team-based flat lattice organization that fosters personal initiative. There are no traditional organizational charts, no chains of command, nor predetermined channels of communication.

Instead, we communicate directly with each other and are accountable to fellow members of our multi-disciplined teams. We encourage hands-on innovation, involving those closest to a project in decision making. Teams organize around opportunities and leaders emerge. This unique kind of corporate structure has proven to be a significant contributor to associate satisfaction and retention."[9]

"Gore is much less formal than most workplaces. Our relationships with other associates are open and informal, and many associates have made lifelong friends with those they met working at Gore....Gore's unique "lattice" structure, which illustrates a nonhierarchical system base on interconnection among associates, is free from traditional bosses and managers. There is no assigned authority, and we become leaders based on our ability to gain the respect of our peers and to attract followers. You will be responsible for managing your own workload and will be accountable to others on your team. More importantly, only you can make a commitment to do something (for example, a task, a project, or a new role)— but once you make a commitment, you will be expected to meet it."[10]

To reinforce the fact that everyone working at Gore is an equal, all employees, including the CEO, are referred to as "associates." In addition, there are no time clocks and the words "boss" and "manager" are considered to be "dirty words." Furthermore, if employees feel that the company is moving in the wrong direction or they believe a decision is wrong, they are expected to speak up and voice their opinion. The goal is that things happen that are in the best overall interest of the company.

In an interview with management expert, Gary Hamel, Gore CEO Terri Kelly had the following to say about the importance of equality: "I think it's wrong to believe that the most important decisions in an enterprise are made by senior leaders. Some of the most impactful decisions at Gore are made by small teams. Within any team you'll find people with very different perspectives; they don't all think alike—and we encourage this. We encourage teams to take a lot of time to come together, to build trust, to build relationships, because we know that if you throw them in a room and they don't have a foundation of trust, it will be chaotic, it will be political, and people will feel as if they're being personally attacked. We invest a lot in making our teams effective, so when they have those great debates—where a scientist doesn't agree with a sales associate, or manufacturing doesn't agree with a product specialist—the debate happens in an environment where everyone is looking for a better solution, versus "you win, I lose."[11]

Given what has just been discussed, it's very clear that the culture at W. L. Gore & Associates is definitely single-status.

Mission—This is What We Do

According to the Gore web site, "Our founder Bill Gore once said, 'The objective of the Enterprise is to make money and have fun doing so.' And we still believe that, more than 50 years later."[12] And, they way they go about the business of making money and having fun is by creating products that are "designed to be the highest quality in their class and revolutionary in their effect."[13] This tells us that Gore is all about innovation—developing cutting edge products rather than "me-too" products. It also tells us that Gore wants its associates to enjoy the ride.

Core Values—This is How We Do It.

At W. L. Gore & Associates, the company's core values are broken into two categories—"Fundamental Beliefs and Guiding Principles."[14] As stated on the Gore web site, "Founder Bill Gore built the company on a set of beliefs and principles that guide us in the decisions we make, in the work we do, and in our behavior toward others. What we believe is the basis for our strong culture, which connects Gore associates worldwide in a common bond."[15] Please note that all parenthetical statements below are those of the authors.

Fundamental Beliefs

- **Belief in the Individual**: If you trust individuals and believe in them, they will be motivated to do what's right for the company. (This reinforces Gore's commitment to a single status culture).

- **Power of Small Teams**: Our lattice organization harnesses the fast decision-making, diverse perspectives, and collaboration of small teams.

- **All in the Same Boat**: All Gore associates are part owners of the company through the associate stock plan. Not only does this allow us to share in the risks and rewards of the company; it gives us an added incentive to stay committed to its long-term success. As a result, we feel we are all in this effort together, and believe we should always consider what's best for the company as a whole when making decisions. (This reinforces the fact that Gore is all about teamwork).

- **Long-Term View**: Our investment decisions are based on long-term payoff, and our fundamental beliefs are not sacrificed for short-term gain.

Guiding Principles

- **Freedom**: The Company was designed to be an organization in which associates can achieve their own goals best by directing their efforts toward the success of the corporation; action is prized; ideas are encouraged; and making mistakes is viewed as part of the creative process. We define freedom as being empowered to encourage each other to grow in knowledge, skill, scope of responsibility, and range of activities. We believe that associates will exceed expectations when given the freedom to do so. (This tells Gore associates that they are free to exercise their autonomy over the performance of their jobs—deciding what to do and how to do it. This provides associates with the opportunity to experience satisfaction of their esteem needs).

- **Fairness**: Everyone at Gore sincerely tries to be fair with each other, our suppliers, our customers, and anyone else with whom we do business.

- **Commitment**: We are not assigned tasks; rather, we each make our own commitments and keep them. (Gore wants its associates to commit only to those work related opportunities where they feel they can experience meaning through their work. This ensures that associates will experience satisfaction of their self-actualization need).

- **Waterline**: Everyone at Gore consults with other associates before taking actions that might be "below the waterline"—causing serious damage to the company.

As you can see, the Gore culture contains all four elements of a *full-engagement* culture. As such, it provides its employees with the opportunity to experience the satisfaction of all five levels of the Maslow need hierarchy. This is why W. L. Gore & Associates experiences such a high level of employee engagement and why it has been made the *Fortune* list of the Top 100 Companies to Work for 17 consecutive years.

Step Two: Hire Only Qualified People Who Mesh With the Culture

Gore goes through great pains to make sure that each new hire is a good fit culturally. According to the Great Place to Work Institute, "Gore has a very low turnover rate....The strength and clarity of the culture at Gore contribute greatly to this low turnover, as does making sure that when a new associate is hired, he or she is right for the culture. At Gore, finding people who can deal with ambiguity, who have a lot of initiative and who can work within the infamous lattice structure is key. Typically five or more associates will interview a candidate, depending upon the role/position that is open, with potential teammates and peers as well as leaders and HR associates participating in the interviews. Extensive reference checks are used to gain a rich understanding of the candidate's work style and values on the job (cultural fit) as much as to explore job qualifications."[16]

Gore also provides some guidance to help prospective employees to assess whether they would be a good fit with the Gore culture. On one of the pages of the Gore web site, the question is asked in bold letters, "Is Gore a good fit for you?" It then goes on to say, "Gore isn't for everyone, but it just may be the best place for you. It's not easy to know whether a company will be a good fit for you and your work style. The questions listed here outline our expectations of Gore associates. Before you apply for an opportunity with Gore, use these questions to honestly evaluate if the qualities we're looking for apply to you."[17]

Do you...

1. Experiment with different approaches or solutions to improve the way things are done?

2. Challenge traditional thinking and identify creative approaches or solutions?

3. Maintain a high standard of performance in uncertain or unstructured situations?

4. Work effectively with others who have different perspectives, talents, backgrounds, and/or styles?

5. Assess your personal strengths and development needs and take responsibility for creating your own development plan to address them?

6. Voice differences of opinion openly and directly?

7. Actively promote collaboration, cooperation, and teamwork to ensure the best business results?

8. Encourage and help others to grow in knowledge, skill, and scope of responsibility?

(The message here is that if you don't think you can find meaning through doing the kinds of things listed above, then you really shouldn't apply for a job at W. L. Gore & Associates.)

The web site also provides links to *Associate Stories* where prospective employees can learn more about the Gore culture and how it affects the day to day work of Gore associates.

The Hiring Process Must be Supported with a Relevant Training and/or Sponsorship Program that Teaches and Reinforces the Culture

According to the Great Place to Work Institute, "Once invited to join the company, a new associate participates in a number of orientation meetings, one during the first month, and others throughout the following months. The first orientation combines a welcome to the Gore culture with an introduction to practical fundamentals. The day-long 'Welcome Aboard' program includes an overview of the cultural principles and practices, as well as basics such as benefits, environmental safety and how to log on to Gore computers and voice mail. Discussions focus on who we are, how we are structured, how we get things done and how Gore may be different from a more traditionally organized company. The differences are of course part of what is attractive about Gore, yet they could be a stumbling block of experienced hires who have already participated in another type of workplace culture.

To address the needs of experience hires, Gore has created a series of programs to help them engage quickly in their work and also learn about the important elements of teamwork and sponsorship that will be crucial to their ability to be successful. Experienced hires are taught about networking opportunities to help them find projects they might want to join. Sponsors of experienced hires (every new associate gets one) are given special training to insure that they can help the experienced hires integrate themselves into the organization.

In some organizations, it's sink or swim when you first get on board, which can lead to a rocky start, higher turnover and project disruptions. Yet when someone has made it through the rigorous screening process and actually landed a job at Gore, sponsors and HR associates want to go all out to make sure that person fits in smoothly so that projects stay on track and teams remain strong."[18]

According to the Gore web site, "Everyone at Gore has a sponsor, who is committed to helping you succeed. Sponsors are responsible for supporting your growth, for providing good feedback on your strengths and areas that offer opportunities for development and for helping you connect with others in the organization."[19] Sponsors also teach new associates how to "navigate" the Gore culture. In an interview with management expert, Gary Hamel, Gore CEO Terri Kelly had this to say about the role of sponsors at Gore: "New associates rely on their sponsors since they don't know how to get things done; they don't know our language. A new associate will probably experience a lot of freedom they didn't have in their last job, but also a lot more responsibility in terms of having to be self-driven and self-initiated. Even though the sponsor is there for you, you need to set your own career goals, and determine for yourself where you can make the biggest contribution. For a lot of people, this is very different from what they would have experienced in a more structured environment."[20]

Step Three: Leaders Must Lead, Not Give Orders

Gore CEO Terri Kelly had this to say about the role of a leader at Gore: "In other companies, the leader is often expected to be the most knowledgeable person on the team, the voice of the company—all-wise and all-knowing. We have a different view. If you want to tap into the whole organization, you have to distribute the responsibility for leadership to the associates who have the relevant knowledge. The Gore model changes the traditional role of the leader. The leader's job is to make sure the culture is healthy: Is it working as a system? Are teams coming together? Are we getting diverse points of view? Are the best ideas rising to the surface? Our leaders have to be comfortable with not being at the center of all the action, with not trying to drive every decision, with not being the most strategic person on the team or the one with the most thoughtful ideas. Their contribution is to help the organization scale and be effective."[21] She later goes on to say, "Our model requires leaders to look at their roles differently. They're not commanders; they're not lynchpins. Their job is to make the rest of the organization successful. They have to give up power and control to allow this chaotic process to happen—so you get diverse perspectives and teams coming together to make decisions."[22]

Above all, leaders at Gore do not tell other associates what to do. As Gary Hamel points out in his book, *The Future of Management*, "During his years at DuPont, Bill Gore developed a keen appreciation for the difference between commitment and compliance. As he often put it, 'Authoritarians cannot impose commitments, only compliance.' Gore believed deeply that willing commitment is many times more valuable to an organization than resigned compliance. This belief is at the heart of another Gore tenet: 'All commitments are self-commitments.' In practice, this means that associates negotiate job assignments with their peers. At Gore, tasks can't be assigned; they can only be accepted....Seasoned executives who join Gore from other companies are initially bewildered by the ethos of voluntary commitment. Those who survive must adapt to life in the lattice. As Steve Young, a consumer-marketing expert hired from Vlasic Foods quickly discovered, 'If you tell anybody what to do here, they'll never work for you again.'"[23]

Conclusion

As you can see, the culture and leadership practices at W. L. Gore & Associates fully embrace all three steps of the Engagement Formula. This has made Gore and extremely successful company and a very desirable place to work.

GOOGLE

Google is a very successful information technology/web search company with more than 50,000 employees working in numerous offices all over the world. It was founded in 1998 by Larry Page and Sergey Brin. According to the Google website, Google has grown by leaps and bounds since then. From offering search in a single language the company now offer dozens of products and services—including various forms of advertising and web applications for all kinds of tasks—in scores of languages. In 2013, Google's revenue was nearly $56 billion. Probably one of the more interesting statistics associated with Google is that it receives well over one million job applications each year and hires only about .05 percent of them. This tells us two very important things about Google: lots of people want to work there and Google is *very particular about who it hires*. Google has made the *Fortune* list of 100 Best Companies to Work For every year since 2007 and has been ranked number one for the last three years in a row. In addition, Google was recently name as The Most Innovative Company in the World by *Fast Company* magazine.

Let's take a look at how the leadership practices at Google match up with the Engagement Formula.

THE ENGAGEMENT FORMULA AT GOOGLE

Step One: Create a Full-Engagement Culture that <u>Defines</u> the Organization and <u>Drives</u> Performance

A full-engagement culture has the following four elements:

Minimal Distractions—So Employees Can Focus on Performing Their Jobs

Employees' physiological and safety needs are very well satisfied at Google. According to the Google web site, "We provide individually-tailored compensation packages that can be comprised of competitive salary, bonus, and equity components, along with the opportunity to earn further financial bonuses and rewards."[1] *CNNMoney* recently quoted a Google spokesperson who said, "...we do believe that competitive compensation plans are important to the future of the company,"[2] In addition, the benefit package at Google is intentionally designed to remove as many day to day distractions as possible for Google employees so they can focus on doing their best work. According to Executive Chairman Eric Schmidt, "The goal is to strip away everything that gets in our employees' way. We provide a standard package of fringe benefits, but on top of that are first-class dining facilities, gyms, laundry rooms, massage rooms, haircuts, carwashes, dry cleaning, commuting buses – just about anything a hardworking employee might want. Let's face it: programmers want to program, they don't want to do their laundry. So we make it easy for them to do both."[3]

Google has the following benefits philosophy: "We strive to be innovative and unique in all services we provide both to customers and employees, including our benefits and perks offerings. We realize and celebrate that our employees have diverse needs, and that this diversity requires flexible and individually directed support. Our priority is to offer a customizable program that can be tailored to the specific needs of each individual, whether they enjoy ice climbing in Alaska, want to retire by age 40, or plan to adopt 3 children."[4]

According to the company web site, the benefits at Google include:[5]

- **Health and wellness:** This includes medical insurance, dental insurance, vision insurance, life and AD & D insurance, short and long term disability insurance and business travel and accident insurance.

- **Retirement and savings:** This includes the Google 401(K) plan. According to the Google web site, "Employees may contribute up to 60% and receive a Google match of up to the greater of (a) 100% of your contribution up to $3,000 or (b) 50% of your contribution up to $8,250 per year with no vesting schedule! We offer a variety of investment options to choose from through Vanguard, our 401(k) Plan Administrator. To help you with those tough investment decisions, employees can access Financial Engines to receive personalized investment advice" and a college savings plan.

- **Time away:** Vacation (this includes 15 days vacation the first year at Google and 25 days the 6th year), holidays (12 paid holidays with sick days taken as necessary), maternity benefits (Up to 12 weeks off at approximately 100% pay, eligible for an additional 6 weeks if employed at Google for more than 1 year) and take-out benefit (To help make things easier, new moms and dads are able to expense up to $500 for take-out meals during the first 3 months that they are home with their new baby).

- **Benefits ... beyond the basics:** This includes things like tuition reimbursement, bonuses for referring someone who accepts a job at Google, back-up child care, gift matching and adoption assistance.

- **Benefits ... way beyond the basics:** These benefits include food (free lunch and dinner cooked by gourmet chefs as snacks between meals), financial planning classes and on-site services at the Mountain View headquarters such as oil change and car wash services, dry cleaning, massage therapy, gym, hair stylist and fitness classes.

Although we could find no hard data, we feel that it's safe to assume that the jobs at Google are very secure for several reasons. First, Google's lifeblood is technology innovation—this is what the company must do to be successful. For this reason, Google invests a lot of time and energy in the hiring process because it wants to make sure that it hires only the smartest and most ambitious people who are nice to work with—people who are motivated by taking on big challenges and problems. These people are passionate and want to throw themselves completely into their jobs. Consequently, they're not going to hire on with a company where they don't think they have a bright future. In addition, Google receives well over one million job applications per year. This wouldn't happen if unless the applicants felt that the jobs at Google were very secure. In addition, Google wouldn't have been ranked number one on the *Fortune* list of 100 Best Companies To Work For during the three most recent years in a row if the jobs there weren't secure.

Google also provides its employees with a very pleasant work environment that is conducive to sharing ideas and opinions. The Google web site describes the offices at Google this way: "Our corporate headquarters, fondly nicknamed the Googleplex, is located in Mountain View, California. Today it's one of our many offices around the globe. While our offices are not identical, they tend to share some essential elements. Here are a few things you might see in a Google workspace:

- Local expressions of each location, from a mural in Buenos Aires to ski gondolas in Zurich, showcasing each office's region and personality.

- Bicycles or scooters for efficient travel between meetings; dogs; lava lamps; massage chairs; large inflatable balls.

- Googlers sharing cubes, yurts and huddle rooms – and very few solo offices.

- Laptops everywhere – standard issue for mobile coding, email on the go and note-taking.

- Foosball, pool tables, volleyball courts, assorted video games, pianos, ping pong tables, and gyms that offer yoga and dance classes.

- Grassroots employee groups for all interests, like meditation, film, wine tasting and salsa dancing.

- Healthy lunches and dinners for all staff at a variety of cafés.

- Break rooms packed with a variety of snacks and drinks to keep Googlers going."[6]

The web site goes on to say, "Though Google has grown a lot since it opened in 1998, we still maintain a small company feel. At lunchtime, almost everyone eats in the office café, sitting at whatever table has an opening and enjoying conversations with Googlers from different teams. Our commitment to innovation depends on everyone being comfortable sharing ideas and opinions."[7]

As the above discussion points out, employees at Google encounter few, if any, distractions that would keep them from giving their full energy and attention to performing their jobs.

Single Status—Everyone is an Equal

Google Executive Chairman, Eric Schmidt, once said in an interview with Steven Pearlstein, financial writer for the *Washington Post*, "No particular person has a strong say….At Google, everyone is the same."[8] In other words, everyone working at Google has the same status. As one Google employee put it, "You have an equal seat at the table, and it's based on the power of your idea, not how long you've been here, tenure, title or anything. In my first week here, I was shocked that for the product I was working on, the product manager was straight out of college. She was making decisions about delaying the product. In every other company I have worked in, it had to go up to three levels of VPs before you could say that you were pushing out the schedule."[9]

It should be noted that at Google, equal status among employees is a necessity not a nicety. The reason is that in order to maintain its innovative edge Google has to hire the smartest and most ambitious people it can find. These are the creative types; the innovators—the people who get off on figuring out how to do the impossible. Furthermore, these are also the kind of people prefer doing things their way, which means they strongly resent being ordered around. According a commentary by Nicholas Carlson on the Pearlstein/Schmidt interview, "...Googlers are a special people to be bossed by no one, only a collective will for good."[10] According to a comment made by Steven Pearlstein in his interview with Eric Schmidt, there is a consensus among Google employees that the managers at Google work for them and not vice versa. Managers then are perceived as leaders whose job it is to provide encouragement and support for the rest of the employees.[11] This is why Google is a network based, flat organization that is very non-hierarchical. It provides employees with the freedom to work on their own terms and do their jobs as they see fit.

Google also prides itself as a consensus culture where everyone committed to finding the *best* idea. The company firmly believes that the *best* idea can only be found if people are willing to openly share their ideas and opinions which often conflict with each other. For this reason, Google encourages lively dissent and debate where employees openly question and challenges each other's ideas. The company has learned that this often very spirited process is what produces the *best* idea. This kind of discussion can only take place in an environment where everyone is an equal and no one has the power to veto which is why Google is committed to its culture of openness, flatness and transparency. As stated on the Google web site, "Because we believe that each Googler is an equally important part of our success, no one hesitates to pose questions directly to Larry or Sergey (the Google founders) in our weekly all-hands ("TGIF") meetings...."[12]

As you can see from the above discussion, the culture at Google is very definitely single-status.

Mission—This is What We Do

According to the Google web site, the mission of the company is to "Google's mission is to organize the world's information and make it universally accessible and useful."[13] Also from the web site, "'The perfect search engine,' says co-founder Larry Page, 'would understand exactly what you mean and give back exactly what you want.' When Google began, you would have been pleasantly surprised to enter a search query and immediately find the right answer. Google became successful precisely because we were better and faster at finding the right answer than other search engines at the time.

But technology has come a long way since then, and the face of the web has changed. Recognizing that search is a problem that will never be solved, we continue to push the limits of existing technology to provide a fast, accurate and easy-to-use service that anyone seeking information can access, whether they're at a desk in Boston or on a phone in Bangkok. We've also taken the lessons we've learned from search to tackle even more challenges."[14] This once again tells us that Google is all about moving forward through technology rather than being content with its past successes.

Core Values—This is How We Do It

Google has a philosophy which is made up of a set of ten core principles that guide the behavior of its employees. Within the context of these principles, Google employees are free to do their jobs as they see fit.

Google Philosophy—Ten Core Principles

As stated on the Google web site, "As we keep looking towards the future, these core principles guide our actions."

The following information regarding Google's ten core principles has been excerpted from the Google web site:[15]

- **Focus on the user and all else will follow.**
  Since the beginning, we've focused on providing the best user experience possible.

- **It's best to do one thing really, really well.**
  We do search. With one of the world's largest research groups focused exclusively on solving search problems, we know what we do well, and how we could do it better.

- **Fast is better than slow.**
  We know your time is valuable, so when you're seeking an answer on the web you want it right away–and we aim to please. We may be the only people in the world who can say our goal is to have people leave our website as quickly as possible.

- **Democracy on the web works.**
  Google search works because it relies on the millions of individuals posting links on websites to help determine which other sites offer content of value.

- **You don't need to be at your desk to need an answer.**
  The world is increasingly mobile: people want access to information wherever they are, whenever they need it.

- **You can make money without doing evil.**
  Google is a business. The revenue we generate is derived from offering search technology to

companies and from the sale of advertising displayed on our site and on other sites across the web.

☐ We don't allow ads to be displayed on our results pages unless they are relevant where they are shown.

☐ We believe that advertising can be effective without being flashy. We don't accept pop–up advertising, which interferes with your ability to see the content you've requested.

☐ Advertising on Google is always clearly identified as a "Sponsored Link," so it does not compromise the integrity of our search results.

- **There's always more information out there.**
  Once we'd indexed more of the HTML pages on the Internet than any other search service, our engineers turned their attention to information that was not as readily accessible.

- **The need for information crosses all borders.**
  Our company was founded in California, but our mission is to facilitate access to information for the entire world, and in every language.

- **You can be serious without a suit.**
  Our founders built Google around the idea that work should be challenging, and the challenge should be fun.

- **Great just isn't good enough.**
  We see being great at something as a starting point, not an endpoint. We set ourselves goals we know we can't reach yet, because we know that by stretching to meet them we can get further than we expected.

As was the case with W. L. Gore & Associates, the culture at Google contains all four elements of a *full-engagement* culture. This means that it provides its employees with the opportunity to experience the satisfaction of all five levels of the Maslow need hierarchy. This explains why Google enjoys such a high level of employee engagement and why it receives well over one million job applications each year.

Step Two: Hire Only Qualified People Who Mesh With the Culture

Google is obsessed with the quality of its employees as well as how they fit into its culture. According to *Corporate Culture Pros*, Google Executive Chairman, Eric Schmidt made the following comment about the hiring philosophy at Google: "Building a company you have the chance to shape the culture. Nothing is more important in doing that than hiring."[16] (Please note that all parenthetical words and phrases throughout the rest of this section on Google are those of the authors.) He went on to make the following points about hiring and culture at Google: "It makes an enormous difference who you hire at every level. Most companies pay lip service to this generically but don't manage that well. You need to get very specific about who is going to succeed in your company....Google spends a lot of time on evaluating technical qualifications, as well as passion and commitment (cultural fit).... Google gives the impression of not managing the company, because they don't. They put all their attention on hiring right people....Once you get started with the right seeding of people; you will see a building of 'self-initiative' behavior....Make sure you have a recruiting team so managers don't just hire their friends."[17]

Steven Levy, author of the best selling *In the Plex: How Google Thinks, Works and Shapes Our Lives* had this to say about the hiring philosophy at Google in an interview with *FINS*: "Everyone has to be really smart and really ambitious. The first thing they do is ask people for their SAT scores and [college] GPAs, which they do no matter how old they are. They think SAT scores are an intelligence quotient and your GPA shows how hard you work. They're looking for someone who's very smart and very ambitious and someone who can survive in the Google atmosphere (culture), where people disagree all the time. The winners are the ones who can produce the most interesting data. There's also the "Googliness" screen, to see if you can fit into the culture. Google has this culture where quirkiness is encouraged but they don't like bad actors, the people who are creepy."[18]

When asked about the role Google's hiring philosophy played in the company's success, Mr. Levy had this to say: "To have a really high bar for intelligence and ambition creates a certain workforce. Lots of people tell me, when they describe what it was like to work at Google, they said when they first got there they were struck by how universally smart all their co-workers are. That's a distinguishing feature of Google—they don't want anyone who's not really smart. The hiring process is made so people won't compromise. For instance, the people who do the hiring aren't hiring for people who are going to work in their groups, that way they're not tempted to say we need someone to fill this position right now and he'll do. They don't want that to happen. Except for a few exceptions, you're not hiring the person who's going to work for you."[19]

The bottom line is that Google is looking for bright people who can think outside the box and work within the Google culture. They want very smart people who are creative, but at the same time who are nice to work with. They don't want any overly arrogant people because they're too hard to work with. According to Eric Schmidt, "It's much easier to have an employee base where everyone is doing exactly what they want every day. They're much easier to manage because they never have any problems. They're always excited, and they're always working on whatever they care about (this means they're able to satisfy their need for meaning through their work). So you're much better off if you select people to work for your firm who really want to change the world—they're doing their life's passion."[20] It should be noted here that when people are doing their life's passion, they're engaged with their work.

As author Steven Levy put it, "Landing a job at Google will put you through a process that makes a Harvard application look easy." [21] According to the Google web site[22] the hiring process begins with an online search for a job opening that interests you by job department, location, or even by key word. Once you find a job opening that interests you, you then apply online. Your qualifications and experience will then be reviewed by one of our recruiters to determine if you are a fit. If you are a possible match for the position, a recruiter will contact you to learn more about your background and answer questions about our hiring process and what it's like to work at Google. If your skills fit the job, a phone interview will be conducted to assess your technical skills and proficiency, to the level of determining whether you should be brought in for in-person interviews. Typically phone interviews are conducted by someone in a similar role and last about 30-40 minutes.

If you are selected of an onsite interview, the interview process for technical positions will evaluate your core software engineering skills including: coding, algorithm development, data structures, design patterns, analytical thinking skills.

During your interview, you'll meet with several engineers across different teams who will give a cross-section view of Google Engineering. Interviewers will ask you questions related to your area of interest and ask you to solve them in real time. The interview process for business and general positions evaluate your problem solving and behavioral abilities. As far as Google is concerned, it's not a question of getting the answer right or wrong, but the process in which you use to solve it. Creativity is important.

Virtually every person who interviews at Google talks to at least four interviewers, drawn from both management and potential colleagues. Everyone's opinion counts, ensuring the hiring process is fair while maintaining high standards as we grow. According to *The Great Workplace,* "While ability and appropriateness to the role are evaluated, so is the candidate's ability to work within the Google culture. Candidates are assessed on their ability to work in a flat organization and on small teams, and the ability to respond to a fast-paced, rapidly changing environment. Successful candidates are passionate, they are willing to attack problems with a flair and creativity, and they have enthusiasm for the challenge of making the world a better place instead of doing evil. A Googley person is ethical and communicates openly, and can be successful without a suit."[23]

Following your interviews, the interviewing team will decide if you are suitable (suitable includes professional competence as well as cultural fit) for the job opening. Google takes hiring very seriously and likes to make consensus-based decisions. To that end, it can take up to two weeks for them to make a definitive decision as to whether they would like to have you join the team.[24]

The Google web site also has advice on how to prepare your resume, prepare for the interview and provides the opportunity to look at the profiles of some Googlers. In addition, in the interest of encouraging qualified people to apply for jobs at Google, the web site provides the following list of The Top Ten Reasons to Work at Google:[25]

1. **Lend a helping hand.** With millions of visitors every month, Google has become an essential part of everyday life – like a good friend – connecting people with the information they need to live great lives.

2. **Life is beautiful.** Being a part of something that matters and working on products in which you can believe is remarkably fulfilling.

3. **Appreciation** is the best motivation, so we've created a fun and inspiring workspace you'll be glad to be a part of, including on-site doctor; massage and yoga; professional development opportunities; shoreline running trails; and plenty of snacks to get you through the day.

4. **Work and play are not mutually exclusive.** It is possible to code and pass the puck at the same time.

5. **We love our employees, and we want them to know it.** Google offers a variety of benefits, including a choice of medical programs, company-matched 401(k), stock options, maternity and paternity leave, and much more.

6. **Innovation is our bloodline.** Even the best technology can be improved. We see endless opportunity to create even more relevant,

more useful, and faster products for our users. Google is the technology leader in organizing the world's information.

7. **Good company everywhere you look.** Googlers range from former neurosurgeons, CEOs, and U.S. puzzle champions to alligator wrestlers and Marines. No matter what their backgrounds, Googlers make for interesting cube mates.

8. **Uniting the world, one user at a time.** People in every country and every language use our products. As such we think, act, and work globally – just our little contribution to making the world a better place.

9. **Boldly go where no one has gone before.** There are hundreds of challenges yet to solve. Your creative ideas matter here and are worth exploring. You'll have the opportunity to develop innovative new products that millions of people will find useful.

10. **There is such a thing as a free lunch after all.** In fact we have them every day: healthy, yummy, and made with love.

The Hiring Process Must be Supported with a Relevant Training and/or Sponsorship Program that Teaches and Reinforces the Culture

According to an article by Amy Lyman of the Great Place to Work Institute, "Leaders and managers at Google seek to ensure that each new hire feels special from the moment they join Google. New hires, called Nooglers, begin their time at Google with an all-day orientation. Speakers come from different departments to talk to the Nooglers, a special tour of the campus is provided, as are folders with benefit information and a coupon for a free massage and discounts for a car wash. At the end of the day, Nooglers are picked up by their mentors and receive a special escort to their work areas where they are greeted with welcome balloons and a bag of chocolates. The Google Buddy (technical person) stops by during the week to ensure each new employee is set up with computers and to assist with any technical questions or concerns. Mentors play a big role in helping Nooglers adjust to the new work environment (this includes the job as well as the Google culture). They stay with their Noogler until they feel completely comfortable and continue as a direct resource for any future needs. To round out the first week, Nooglers are recognized at weekly TGIF events, with their names and what group they work in shown on a large screen. They also get their first chance to feel part of Google as they sit in the front rows as Google founders Larry and Sergey talk shop. A few employee comments confirm the success of Google's welcoming activities: 'I was really impressed with the openness and amount of information given to Nooglers during orientation and throughout the first week.' 'I couldn't believe all the speakers that take time to come and speak to Nooglers during the first day orientation.' 'My group had a special orientation where I was introduced to my group. It really made me feel special.'"[26] What all this means is that Google does a pretty thorough job of orienting its new employees to their jobs as well as on how to navigate the Google culture.

Step Three: Leaders Must Lead, Not Give Orders

As former CEO Eric Schmidt put it, "Google is run by its culture, not by me."[27] The company is organized from the bottom up which means the role of managers and executives is to provide encouragement and support to the people who are doing the work. He goes on to say, "People are doing what they think best and they tolerate having us (managers and executives) around....Part of the job of being the CEO in a company like Google is to have an environment where people are constantly throwing you their best ideas as opposed to being afraid to talk to you."[28]

An article by Roslyn Frenz which appeared on *eHow*.com states that "...Google has always operated on the motto, 'Don't be evil.' This moral code helps to guide employees because Google only holds them accountable to management to a degree. To keep the spirit of innovation the company was founded on; Google employees are mostly accountable to themselves. They have the freedom to spend 70 percent of their time on current assignments, 20 percent on related projects of their choosing, and 10 percent on new projects in any area they desire.... Google executives encourage employees and managers to work directly with each other, instead of through more formal channels.... Instead of setting goals for them, Google's management helps their employees meet the objectives that the employees set for themselves. The company sees its managers as leaders who facilitate inspiration and empower employees....Although Google's management makes suggestions, employees use metrics that they choose themselves to measure their progress toward their goals. Supervisors act as managers to ensure that the employees meet their own goals, but employees see them as leaders because the employees themselves set the benchmarks....The Company's leadership allows employees to change the parameters of their jobs when needed. Employees are encouraged to be their own leaders, evaluate their jobs and then propose better ways to do their jobs. Google's leaders want their employees to 'think out loud,' and have open discussions about their goals and plans for achievement. The structure promotes corporate transparency because employees are able to witness and contribute to the leadership function. As a result, almost every employee has access to almost any managerial meeting. Google's management realizes that every employee has a stake in the company and employees in turn feel a responsibility for the outcome of the company's projects.... Google's methods attract top talent because their management focuses on controlling through shared vision. Where many companies have bureaucratic and linear controls, Google allows employees to set and maintain their own standards. These open policies translate into a distinctive corporate structure that inspires good nature and guidance. Employees love to work at Google, but not just because of perks such as flexible work time and bonuses, they also love the work that comes from the cross-functional leadership structure."[29] The bottom line at Google then is that leaders truly function as leaders, they don't give orders.

CONCLUSION

It's very clear that the culture and leadership practices at Google fully embrace all three steps of the Engagement Formula. This has not only made Google and extremely successful company, but a very desirable place to work as well.

SAS

SAS is the world's largest privately held software company. It's the leader in business analytics software and services and the largest independent vendor in the business intelligence market. The company was founded in 1976 by Anthony Barr, Jim Goodnight, John Sall and Jane Helwig. Jim Goodnight has served as the company's CEO from day one through the present. SAS has over 14,000 employees working in more than 400 offices in 56 countries and last year's revenue was more than $3 billion. Probably the most interesting statistic associated with SAS is that its voluntary turnover rate of employees is only two percent while the industry average ranges between 15 and 20 percent. This tells us that people absolutely love working at SAS. This also helps explain why SAS is the only company besides W. L. Gore & Associates to make the *Fortune* list of the Top 100 Companies To Work For 17 consecutive years. SAS has also made the lists of the best places to work in Norway, Australia, Belgium, Brazil, Canada, Switzerland, Finland, France, Germany, India, Italy, Korea, Mexico, Netherlands, Poland, Portugal Spain, The Netherlands and Sweden.

Let's take a look at the leadership practices of SAS and see how they match up with the Engagement Formula.

THE ENGAGEMENT FORMULA AT SAS

Step One: Create a Full-Engagement Culture that <u>Defines</u> the Organization and <u>Drives</u> Performance

A full-engagement culture has the following four elements:

Minimal Distractions—So Employees Can Focus on Performing Their Jobs

SAS employees' physiological and safety needs are very well satisfied. Compensation at SAS includes a competitive base salary which means SAS employees are paid very well. According to The Great Place to Work Institute, salaries are determined by matching market data to job titles.[1] The compensation package at SAS also includes bonuses and profit sharing.[2]

According to the SAS web site, "The company offers a wide range of benefits to reduce stress and distraction, and let employees focus on their work."[3] The SAS benefit package does just that. According to the Best Place To Work Institute, SAS estimates that the average employee's total benefit package is equivalent to more than 40% of his or her salary.[4] As Justine Costigan put it in an article which appeared on *Forbescustom.com*, SAS's strategy is to offer more than the industry norm in terms of benefits.[5] The article goes on to quote Kristen Vosburgh, the Vice President of Compensation and Benefits at SAS, as saying, "We are always benchmarking ourselves and making sure we stay in the top tier of companies in terms of benefits. We always strive to be leading edge."[6]

From their web site, SAS has this to say about their benefits package: "Our employees are among our greatest assets. SAS' unique, award-winning work environment is designed to nurture and encourage creativity, innovation and quality. We think it's a challenging, employee-friendly and fun place to work. So do a lot of other people, including FORTUNE magazine, Forbes and the authors of the books, *Guts!* and *Companies that Care*. Why do we invest so much in our employees? Because it's the right thing to do and it makes great business sense."[7]

According to the company web site, the benefits at SAS are broken down into the following categories:[8]

Your Career

We value the employee-friendly culture that we have created over the years, and believe that we have some of the best employees in America. In keeping with that belief, we offer the following:

- Excellent Working Environment

- Casual Dress Code

- Training and Development Opportunities

- Career Advancement Opportunities

Your Time

Having a balanced life means that you spend some time away from work. That's why we give our employees the time they need to lead a well-balanced life. Whether through our paid time-off plans, or our flexibility in scheduling, we strive to meet the needs of our employees.

- Company Paid Vacation – Three weeks per year to start and four weeks per year after 10 years of employment

- Paid Sick Days

- Flexible Work Schedules (subject to manager's approval)

- 11 Paid Holidays

- Jury Duty, Military and Funeral Leaves

Your Finances

How are you going to meet your future financial goals? That can be an important consideration when deciding where to work. At SAS, it's not just about the pay; we also want to help you plan for your future.

- Competitive Pay

- Company-Paid Life Insurance

- SAS Retirement Plan, including Profit Sharing, 401(k) and Rollovers

- Retiree Health Reimbursement Arrangement (HRA) – a health care spending account for eligible retirees

- Financial, Retirement and Estate Planning seminars offered on-site

Your Health

We want to help our employees lead healthy and productive lives. For that reason, our benefit offerings are among the finest anywhere.

- Comprehensive Medical, Dental and Vision Plans provided to full-time and part-time employees

- Health Care Flexible Spending Account

- Short- and Long-Term Disability Plans

- On-Site Health Care Centers at Cary, NC and Austin, TX offices, offering a vast array of health care services and programs for employees and their family members covered by a SAS health plan

- On-Site Recreation and Fitness Center at Cary headquarters and Fitness Center reimbursements for regional office employees

- Employee Assistance Program (EAP) for confidential assistance with personal matters

Your Family

At SAS, we understand the importance of leading a well-balanced life and meeting family needs and obligations. We offer the following benefits to help you maintain this balance:

- Dependent Care Flexible Spending Accounts

- Domestic Partner Benefits

- Adoption Assistance

- Family Medical Leave

- Family Sick Days

- Paid Paternity Leave

- Flexible Work Schedules (subject to manager's approval)

- Subsidized, On-Site Child Care Centers in Cary for children of employees with at least one year of service (as space is available) and subsidized child care in regional offices. Eligibility is based on seniority, and there is normally a waiting list for this popular and valuable benefit.

- Competitively priced, on-site Summer Camp in Cary for school-age children

- College Scholarship Program to encourage the education and careers of children of SAS employees

- Work/Life Resources available to assist employees with a variety of family-related issues

Your Extras

Who doesn't like a little something extra? Over the years, we have developed relationships with vendors to offer discounts and services that our employees really value, such as:

- Group Rates for auto, home, renter, long-term care and supplemental life insurance with payroll deduction

- Group-Rate Tickets to events

- Dozens of Vendor Discounts for SAS employees

- Many On-Site Vendor Services offered in Cary and regional locations

As Jenn Mann, VP of Human Resources put it, "SAS' philosophy of reducing distractions helps keep employees engaged and focused and increases productivity."[9]

The jobs at SAS are very secure. According to an article by Rebecca Leung which appeared on *cbsnews.com*, SAS has never laid off a single employee.[10] In January, 2009, at the height of the recent recession, company cofounder, Jim Goodnight became aware of the growing concern among employees over the possibility of job cuts. To allay their fears, he filmed a companywide webcast that contained a promise. "I told them we would have no layoffs for the entire year—but that I needed them to pitch in and reduce expenses, to slow down hiring and cut it out completely if possible. Everybody did pitch in and productivity actually went up in 2009...It was one of our top three most profitable years."[11] In a company press release regarding the same issue, Mr. Goodnight said, "I wanted them to stay focused on customer needs and not be distracted by issues related to corporate viability. The result is that we continued to grow in the downturn and we are ready to launch exciting new products in 2010. The momentum is greater than it's ever been for this company."[12] He then proceeded to make the same no-layoff promise for 2010. Mr. Goodnight fully understands that employees will take care of the company that takes care of them. During a tough economy, SAS did not waver in its commitment to its employees.

SAS provides its employees with an extremely pleasant work environment. According to *knowledge@wharton.com*, "(Mr.) Goodnight said his ideas about an employee-friendly environment developed after a year spent working in Florida for the Apollo space project in the 1960s, where staffers 'were treated like workers on an assembly line.' After founding SAS, Goodnight insisted that workers not only get individual offices (he didn't like cubicles when he worked on the Apollo project), but also break rooms stocked with free refreshments, on-site gymnasiums and day care centers, and a team of company physicians and nurses."[13] Today the SAS "campus" is second to none in terms of its amenities which include a baby grand piano in the company cafeteria, more than 3,000 pieces of art which are displayed throughout the campus,[14] athletic fields, tennis courts, basketball and racquetball courts, a swimming pool and a full gym. According to author, Nigel Barber, "Keeping employees happy has certainly paid off for SAS with a 40-fold increase in revenues since 1984 based on holding a niche in the software industry that is immune from competition. Treating employees well is a profitable strategy because they reciprocate by working hard. In fact, employees are so strongly motivated that they sometimes describe the campus as a golden cage that they never want to leave."[15] This strong focus on employee well-being has resulted in an employee turnover rate of two percent[16] in an industry where the norm is 22 percent.[17] As Jenn Mann, vice president of human resources puts it, "You are not going to succeed unless you have a stable workforce....we estimate it (SAS's low employee turnover rate) is saving the company hundreds of millions (of dollars)...."[18] This is money that competing companies have to spend recruiting and training new employees.

One of the more interesting aspects of the SAS work environment is the "flexible" 35 hour work week. A programmer himself, Jim Goodnight understands first-hand the issues his employees have to deal with. He knows that tired programmers who stay at work late make mistakes that they have to spend costly time correcting the next day. For this reason, he instituted the "flexible" 35 hour work week. Mr. Goodnight feels it's better that employees go home and spend time with their families rather than staying at the office making a lot of mistakes. Speaking to the flexible work schedule, Jenn Mann had this to say in *The Great Workplace*, "Creativity is especially important to SAS because software is a product of the mind. Creativity doesn't come on demand. We're all inspired at different times. At SAS, we create a stimulating and flexible work environment that allows employees to work when they are most innovative and productive."[19]

As the above discussion points out, SAS employees encounter few, if any, distractions that would keep them from giving all their energy and attention to performing their jobs.

Single Status—Everyone is an Equal

SAS has no formal organizational structure. Rather its culture is one of openness and informality where employees have a high degree of autonomy over the performance of their jobs. According to Mohan Thite, author of *Managing People in the New Economy*, SAS is a place where *all* people are treated fairly and equally.[20] Managers function as leaders where the emphasis is on coaching and mentoring rather than monitoring and controlling. Mr. Thite goes on to say, "In its practices and day to day operations, the company is a very egalitarian place. Neither Jim Goodnight (the company CEO) nor anyone else has a reserved parking space. His healthcare plan is no different from that of the day care workers. There is no executive dining room—everyone regardless of his or her position can eat at one of the on-site cafeterias, where high-quality, subsidized food is accompanied by a pianist playing during the lunch hour....Dress is casual and decided by what the person feels comfortable wearing."[21]

As is the case with Google, equal status among employees is not a nicety, it's a necessity. The reason is that in order for SAS to continue its incredible track record of success it must be able to attract and retain bright, creative and ambitious people who get excited about solving difficult problems. These are the kind of people who resent being told what to do because they prefer doing things their way. Furthermore, if they can't do things their way, they will quickly leave and go to work for another company. SAS' two percent employee turnover rate shows that this clearly is not the case. This is why the underlying managerial philosophy at SAS is one of "give people what they need to do their job and then get out of their way." In addition managers at SAS are actively involved in the day to day operations of the company. For example, Jim Goodnight, in addition to being CEO, still spends time doing programming and leading product development teams.

Another way that SAS demonstrates that everyone is of equal status is by the way it handles compensation and employment status. According to the Great Place To Work Institute, "All SAS regular non-exempt employees (full time and part-time) are paid on a salaried basis for their regular work schedule; and they receive additional pay for hours worked beyond their normal work schedule. Only substitutes and students are paid by the hour. And all salaries at SAS are set in the same way—by matching market data to the job title....All staff who might be contracted out in other organizations—gardeners, food service employees, healthcare staff—are SAS employees. So not only do non-exempt workers receive a salary which provides income security as opposed to the variability of hourly pay, all people who work at SAS are employees and are included in the SAS community, sharing in the benefits and contributing to its strength. The health plans available to service workers are the same ones available to senior leaders. It's the same with childe-care services, fitness programs, food service, etc....The message the practices send is that everyone belongs and is a full member of the organization. These practices reinforce the founding philosophy, affirming that every employee is important and can make a difference."[22]

From the above discussion, it's very clear that SAS has a single-status culture.

Mission—This is What We Do

The Mission of SAS Institute is as follows: "SAS delivers proven solutions that drive innovation and improve performance."[23] According to Jim Goodnight, "We've worked hard to create a corporate culture that is based on trust between employees and the company—a culture that rewards innovation, encourages employees to try new things and yet doesn't penalize them for taking chances and a culture that cares about employees personal and professional growth."[24] This has resulted in a very happy workforce which, in turn, has resulted in a very happy and satisfied customer base.

SAS is very proud of the fact that during the recent tough economic times it has been able to live up to its *enduring commitment.* According to a recent Corporate Social Responsible Report, "...SAS was able to retain economic growth, maintain a low employee turnover rate in a world-class work environment and continue investing in efforts to mitigate the environmental impact of its operations."[25] SAS also strongly believes in giving back to the community—especially in the area of education.[26] In other words, the goal at SAS is not just to make money, but to make it in an ethical way that makes the world a better place. As such, its employees are provided the opportunity to make a difference in company that makes a difference. This helps explain the extremely low turnover rate at SAS—the work there is very much worth doing.

Core Values—This is How We Do It

According to the company web site, SAS refers to its core values as *guiding principles*. These principles guide the day to day decisions and behavior of all SAS employees. These principles are presented below:[27] (Please note that the parenthetical statements below are those of the authors.)

- **Approachable**
  The company strives to be approachable, so customers recognize SAS as a reliable partner and not just a vendor. (Customers must feel welcome when they approach SAS with ideas for new products and suggestions for existing products.)

- **Customer-Driven**
  SAS is about being customer-driven, engaging with customers to find out what they want and helping to solve their problems. (SAS does not have a long range plan for developing new products. Instead, it relies on customer input for new product ideas.)

- **Swiftness and Agility**
  Swiftness and agility are required to adapt to changing technology and global conditions. (There's no such thing as resting on past success at SAS. The company operates in a fast paced business environment of changing technology and global conditions.)

- **Innovative**
  SAS relies on the kind of innovation that grows in a workplace culture where employees feel valued, vested and inspired. (New products are developed internally; they are not acquired. This provides

SAS employees with continuous supply of new and interesting work opportunities.)

- **Trustworthy**
  SAS demands that as a company, it must be trustworthy, an ethical business partner that customers can count on for their critical decision-making processes. (In other words, SAS seeks to make money in ethical ways that make its customers better off.)

Within the context of SAS' enduring commitment and core values then, employees are free to do their jobs as they see fit—deciding what to do and how to do it. This is the kind of environment where bright, creative and ambitious people absolutely thrive.

As you can see, the culture at SAS contains all four elements of a *full- engagement* culture. As such, SAS provides its employees with the opportunity to satisfy all five levels of the Maslow need hierarchy. This explains why it has been ranked number one on the *Fortune* list of the Top 100 Companies To Work For during 2010 and 2011, number three in 2012 and number two in 2013 and 2014.

Step Two: Hire Only Qualified People Who Mesh With the Culture

Like all companies with a high level of employee engagement, SAS uses its culture as the primary criterion for hiring new employees. As mention earlier, if employees are to become engaged with their work, there must be a good fit between those individuals and the mission and values of the organization. In other words, they must be able to satisfy their need for meaning through working at that particular organization. This is what makes people passionate about what they do. According to the Great Place To Work Institute, "As is true in all great workplaces, people at SAS take special care during the recruiting and hiring process to insure that they find the best people to join their organization. And what does the 'best' mean for SAS? They certainly look for people with specific job skills, yet more importantly they are looking for people with characteristics that parallel the company's five values. Employees are expected to be approachable, to focus on customer needs, to be swift and agile, innovative and trustworthy. While these qualities are certainly things many companies strive to find in their new employees, SAS does it very successfully."[28]

According to the company web site, "SAS' success as a company and reputation as a best-in-class workplace, help it attract the best and the brightest candidates. We focus on hiring talented individuals with the right knowledge, skills and cultural fit who have the same spirit of innovation and creativity and who thrive on challenging work. The culture at SAS is linked directly to its values and core competencies. This leads to dedicated, loyal employees who develop leading-edge solutions for customers. In 2013, SAS received more than 59,000 resumes for 328 positions.

SAS recruiters develop position-related, competency-based questions and culture-fit questions that are based on the company's values. Teamwork and collaboration are part of our daily life at SAS. In order to ensure a good fit with the team, candidates also participate in team interviews. This often gives candidates an even better picture of the corporate culture and offers a glimpse into life as a SAS employee."[29]

The Hiring Process Must be Supported with a Relevant Training and/or Sponsorship Program that Teaches and Reinforces the Culture

According to the Great Place To Work Institute, "What is unique about hiring at SAS is another perspective that is incorporated into the recruitment and on-boarding process. A specific guiding philosophy about people has influenced the organization from the beginning – 'if you treat people as if they make a difference to the company, then they will make a difference to the company'. So at SAS, people are brought in with the clear expectation that they will make a difference – every single person."[30] The formal on-boarding process at SAS lasts about 90 days, is very high-touch where people are made to feel valued and emphasizes the company's core values. New employees are assigned a "buddy" to show them, how to navigate the company and its culture.[31]

"To ensure that employees take full advantage of their work experiences, SAS offers skills development, employee support, direct contact with managers, directors and the CEO as well as feedback surveys. As a result of our policies, we have a low staff turnover." [32] As was mentioned earlier, the most recent figure for employee turnover at SAS was two percent. Obviously they do a very good job when it comes to hiring new employees or it would be much higher than that as the industry average hovers around 15-20 percent.

Step Three: Leaders Must Lead, Not Give Orders

From the above discussion, it's very apparent that the leaders at SAS lead; they don't spend their time telling employees what to do and how to do it. Co-founder and CEO

Jim Goodnight has long been a proponent of *servant leadership* where the role of the leader is to support and encourage the people he or she is leading. As mentioned earlier, managers at SAS function as *leaders* where the emphasis is on empowering and coaching rather than monitoring and controlling. Their job is to give people what they need to do their job and then get out of their way. In addition, if leaders did try to give orders to the bright, creative and ambitious type of people that SAS tries to recruit, hire and retain, they would quickly move on to another company.

CONCLUSION

It's very clear that the culture and leadership practices at SAS fully embrace the Engagement Formula. This has resulted in SAS being an extremely desirable place to work and an remarkably successful company.

SOUTHWEST AIRLINES

According to the company web site, Southwest Airlines is a publicly traded company that was incorporated in Texas and commenced Customer Service on June 18, 1971, with three Boeing 737 aircraft serving three Texas cities—Houston, Dallas, and San Antonio. Today, Southwest operates 680 Boeing aircraft among 96 cities and has nearly 45,000 employees—most of whom are unionized. Southwest topped the monthly domestic originating passenger rankings for the first time in May 2003. Yearend results for 2013 marked Southwest's 41st consecutive year of profitability. Southwest became a major airline in 1989 when it exceeded the billion-dollar revenue mark. Southwest is the United States' most successful low fare, high frequency, point-to-point carrier. Southwest operates more than 3,600 flights a day coast-to-coast, making it the largest U.S. carrier based on domestic passengers carried as of December 31, 2010.[1]

Southwest has long been considered the poster child on how to run a highly successful business. Its employees absolutely love working there, are amazingly loyal and provide incredible levels of customer service which has given rise to legendary stories like the following which was reported in *Business Week* on March 5, 2007:

"Bob Emig was flying home from St. Louis on Southwest Airlines this past December when an all-too-familiar travel nightmare began to unfold. After his airplane backed away from the gate, he and his fellow passengers were told the plane would need to be de-iced. When the aircraft was ready to fly two and a half hours later, the pilot had reached the hour limit set by the Federal Aviation Administration, and a new pilot was required. By that time, the plane had to be de-iced again. Five hours after the scheduled departure time, Emig's flight was finally ready for takeoff. A customer service disaster, right? Not to hear Emig tell it. The pilot walked the aisles, answering questions and offering constant updates. Flight attendants, who Emig says 'really seemed like they cared,' kept up with the news on connecting flights. And within a couple of days of arriving home, Emig, who travels frequently, received a letter from Southwest that included two free round-trip ticket vouchers. 'I could not believe they acknowledged the situation and apologized," says Emig. "Then they gave me a gift, for all intents and purposes, to make up for the time spent sitting on the runway.' Emig's 'gift' from the airline was not the result of an unusually kind customer service agent who took pity on his plight. Nor was it a scramble to make amends after a disastrous operational fiasco....Rather, it was standard procedure for Southwest Airlines."[2]

Southwest topped the very first list of the *Fortune* 100 Best Companies To Work For in 1998 and has made the list several times since. Last year it was ranked number one on Glassdoor's Best Place to Work list. In addition, Southwest has won numerous customer service awards and distinctions and regularly appears on the *Bloomberg Businessweek* list of Customer Service Champs. Southwest is also a very desirable place to work. In 2013 Southwest received 100,682 resumes and hired 1,521 new Employees.[3]

Let's take a look at the leadership practices of Southwest Airlines and see how they match up with the Engagement Formula.

THE ENGAGEMENT FORMULA AT SOUTHWEST AIRLINES

Step One: Create a Full-Engagement Culture that <u>Defines</u> the Organization and <u>Drives</u> Performance

A full-engagement culture has the following four elements:

Minimal Distractions—So Employees Can Focus on Performing Their Jobs

Southwest employees' physiological and safety needs are very well satisfied. Southwest has always espoused that *employees come first*—if you treat your employees right, they'll treat your customers right which means they'll come back again and again and this is what makes shareholders happy. Treating employees right at Southwest begins with paying them equitably. As company cofounder Herb Kelleher said when he was CEO, "You can't have a culture of commitment and performance without equitable employee compensation…"[4] This is why Southwest strives to pay its employees at or above average pay levels within the industry.[5] As CEO Gary Kelly said in an interview with CBS' *Sunday Morning* correspondent Martha Teichner, when speaking about Southwest, "It's never had a layoff. It's never cut salaries. In fact, it's one of the best-paid, most highly-unionized airlines in the industry."[6] It turns out Mr. Kelly is right. According to the Centre for Asia Pacific Aviation's *America Airline Daily*, Southwest has the highest wage/benefit package of all US Airlines.[7] So from a compensation standpoint, Southwest employees are well taken care of.

Southwest also offers a very generous package of benefits. According to the company site, benefits at Southwest are broken into the following categories:[8]

The Freedom to Create Financial Security

As an Employer, Southwest knows that financial security is a top priority for our People. We offer great programs like these to help our Employees plan for the future.

- **401(k) Plan:** This Company-sponsored retirement plan allows Employees to contribute a portion of their pay on a pre-tax basis to build up savings for retirement. Currently, we match Employee contributions $1 for $1 up to 9.3 percent of eligible salary.

- **ProfitSharing Plan:** Without great Employees, we wouldn't have great profits. Each year Southwest rewards our People with a portion of the Company's profits to Employee ProfitSharing accounts. For example, in 2006 Southwest contributed 7.96 percent of our Employees' salaries into their ProfitSharing accounts!

- **Employee Stock Purchase Plan:** This plan allows Employees to buy shares of Southwest stock at a 10% discount.

The Freedom to Pursue Good Health

"An apple a day keeps the doctor away..." but in case it doesn't, Southwest has you covered! Our competitive health package makes staying healthy affordable, currently for as little as $15 per month.

- Medical

- Vision

- Dental

- Life Insurance

- Other Benefits
  - ☐ Long-term Disability Insurance
  - ☐ Dependent Care Spending Account
  - ☐ Healthcare Spending Account
  - ☐ Adoption Assistance Reimbursement Benefit
  - ☐ Child and Elder Care Resource and Referral Program
  - ☐ Mental Health Chemical Dependency/Employee Assistance Program

The Freedom to Travel

"You are now free to move about the country"...and so are Southwest Employees. Our Employees enjoy many great travel perks:

- **Free Flights on Southwest Airlines**
  Employees, spouses, eligible dependent children, and parents fly Southwest for free. Committed/Registered Partners also enjoy travel privileges on Southwest. Space-available travel is unlimited and starts on day one of employment.

- **Discounted Flights**
  Discounted, space-available travel with

participating carriers is available through the Southwest Airlines Pass Bureau, subject to eligibility and other restrictions.

- **Buddy Passes**
  Our Buddy Pass Program provides a way for Employees to share the Freedom to Travel with friends and family not covered under dependent flight privileges. Employees can earn up to four passes per quarter based on hours worked. The Employee is responsible for applicable taxes.

- **Additional Discounts**
  Many companies including hotels, theme parks, and rental car companies offer discounts to Southwest Airlines Employees.

The Freedom to Learn and Grow

Southwest Airlines values our People and their goals. These are just a few of the many opportunities to learn and grow our Employees are provided.

- **Learning**
  □ University for People: Our state-of-the-art training facility provides professional and personal development for our Employees.
  □ Leadership Training: Want to be a Leader? Classes like Leadership 101 and Leadership Southwest Style will show you how!
  □ Personal Development: The University offers classes on interviewing, public speaking, and everything in between.
  □ Initial and Recurrent Training: Southwest ensures that each and every Employee receives thorough training.

- **Growing**
  □ Moving around the Company: Southwest LUVs to promote from within. We encourage movement around the Company to increase skills and Company knowledge.
  □ Days in the Field: Interested in another department or position? Spend some time in another person's shoes learning about their job.
  □ Manager in Training (MIT) Program: Our MIT Program was formed to identify and develop Leaders.

The Freedom to Make a Positive Difference

We're not known as the LUV airline for nothing! Making a positive difference is part of what keeps our Culture alive. Employees are encouraged to Share the Spirit of Southwest through programs like these:

- **Spread the LUV:** Southwest Employees filled our Headquarters lobby with donated jars of peanut butter.

- **Employee Catastrophic Fund:** Employees have the option of making payroll deducted donations to this fund supporting our own Employees in times of trouble. In the aftermath of Hurricane Katrina, Employees donated $543,300 to Fellow Employees in need.

- LUV Classic Golf Tournaments: Southwest sponsors annual golf tournaments in Dallas and Phoenix. Since the tradition started, Southwest raised over $9.7 million for Ronald McDonald Houses.

- **Adopt-A-Pilot:** Many of our Pilots volunteer their time visiting fifth grade classes and corresponding with students throughout the year. The program allows students to see the importance of education in reaching personal goals.

- **Operation Phone Home:** Southwest partnered with the USO and its OPERATION PHONE HOME program to provide phone cards to troops.

The Freedom to Work and Have Fun

Happy Employees = Happy Customers. Happy Customers keep Southwest flying. Our one of a kind culture includes FUN events like these that keep our Employees motivated and make it worthwhile to work hard for the Company they love!

- **Haunted Headquarters:** Halloween is more spectacular than spooky at this annual event. Skits, costumes, and activities provide FUN for our Employees, families, and friends.

- **Culture Committees:** These Employee-led groups volunteer time to celebrate life events, plan FUN events, and make Southwest a FUN place to work.

- **Chili Cookoff:** Our annual event featuring food, talent, prizes, and of course, chili!

- **Spirit Parties:** Events hosted by our field locations which help promote cross-country FUN!

The Freedom to Stay Connected

Being a Southwest Employee makes you part of the Southwest family! As our Company grows, we know how important it is to keep those family ties. We have many communication methods in place to do just that.

- **Today@SWA:** Our daily newsletter that provides late-breaking news, Company announcements, messages from Leaders, industry news, Employee recognition, and more.

- **Employee Communications:** An entire Team dedicated to keeping us informed and in touch.

- **LUVLines:** Our Employee magazine published monthly features in-depth articles on Company and industry news.

- **Message to the Field:** Our traveling annual meeting offers Employees the opportunity to hear a Company update from our CEO and other Executive Leaders.

- **SWALife:** Our secure Employee web site that provides important Company News and Information, Culture Updates, Employee Benefits, Travel Tools, and other business-critical content.

- **SWA Blog:** Nuts About Southwest is a blog all about our Employees, Customers, airplanes, and airports. We really are Nuts about Southwest and we hope that our Readers are too.

- **Employee News Line:** Gary Kelly and other Southwest Officers record a recap of what's important at Southwest on this toll-free hotline.

To say that the jobs at Southwest are very secure is an understatement—the company has never laid off a single employee! As cofounder Herb Kelleher put it when he was CEO, "Our most important tools for building employee partnership are job security and a stimulating work environment. Our union leadership has recognized that we provide job security, and there hasn't been a lot of that in the airline industry. Certainly there were times when we could have made substantially more profits in the short term if we had furloughed people, but we didn't. We were looking at our employees' and our company's longer-term interests. And, as it turns out, providing job security imposes additional discipline, because if your goal is to avoid layoffs, then you hire very sparingly. So our commitment to job security has actually helped us keep our labor force smaller and more productive than our competitors'."[9]

This commitment to a no-layoff policy is reinforced in CEO Gary Kelly's most recent message to the company's stakeholders: "For the U.S. airline industry, the first decade of this century will forever be known as the 'lost decade'—fewer passengers, fewer flights, fewer airplanes, and fewer aviation jobs. Faced with the worst economic recession in aviation history, a worldwide credit crisis, and astronomical jet fuel prices, the airline industry endured billions of lost dollars and numerous bankruptcies and liquidations. And yet, while not immune to the economic collapse, brutal competition, and energy price volatility, Southwest Airlines prevailed. We emerged from the worst decade in aviation history without bankruptcy, without furloughs, without pay cuts, and without degradation of our Customer Experience. We even conquered a feat unmatched in U.S. aviation history, with 2010 marking our 38th consecutive year of profitability. ... We credit our success to our Employees, who are our most valuable asset and our competitive advantage. Their Warrior Spirit helped us emerge victoriously through the 'lost decade.' Our audacious People create a FUN travel experience, respond with compassion when travel plans change, generate innovative ideas that enhance the Customer Experience, and donate their time and LUV to those who need it."[10]

Most of Southwest's employees work in and around planes and airports in 72 cities throughout the US. In addition there are Customer Service and Support Centers in Albuquerque, Chicago, Houston, Phoenix, Oklahoma City and San Antonio with a headquarters near Love Field in Dallas. What makes the work environment pleasant and at Southwest is not so much the aesthetic surroundings, rather it's the family atmosphere where employees genuinely care about each other, look out for each other and work together as a team in an exciting industry where there's almost never a dull moment. For these reasons, employees absolutely love coming to work at Southwest. This is a big reason why Southwest enjoys an employee turnover rate that is well below the industry average and why 100,682 people applied for jobs there this past year.

As the above discussion illustrates, Southwest employees encounter few, if any, distractions that would keep them from giving all their energy and attention to performing their jobs.

Single Status—Everyone is Treated as an Equal

At Southwest, employees are not told what to do and how to do it by a boss. Rather they are expected to exercise their freedom over their jobs and act in the best interest of the company. As Herb Kelleher put it when he was CEO, "...it's not enough to assure people a job, equally important is allowing them to feel liberated when they come to work, to be creative, to think outside the lines."[11] Southwest has always stressed leadership (employee freedom) over management (employee control). As Mr. Kelleher once said, "A financial analyst once asked me if I was afraid of losing control of our organization. I told him I've never had control and I never wanted it. If you create an environment where the people truly participate, you don't need control. They know what needs to be done, and they do it....We're not looking for blind obedience. We're looking for people who on their own initiative want to be doing what they're doing because they consider it to be a worthy objective. I have always believed that the best leader is the best server. And if you're a servant, by definition you're not controlling."[12] In addition, at Southwest, there are no formal channels of communication—employees are free to communicate directly with whomever they need to on a first name basis. Furthermore, hierarchy and titles are downplayed and elitism is frowned upon.

From the above discussion, it's very clear that Southwest has a single-status culture. To reinforce its single-status culture, the following commitment to its employees is published on its web site: "We are committed to provide our Employees a stable work environment with equal opportunity for learning and personal growth. Creativity and innovation are encouraged for improving the effectiveness of Southwest

Airlines. Above all, Employees will be provided the same concern, respect, and caring attitude within the organization that they are expected to share externally with every Southwest Customer."[13]

Mission—This is What We Do

According to the company's web site, "The mission of Southwest Airlines is dedication to the highest quality of Customer Service delivered with a sense of warmth, friendliness, individual pride, and Company Spirit."[14] In other words, the goal of Southwest is to deliver the absolute *best* and most heartfelt customer service possible. As stated on its web site, "Our Employees listen to our Customers' needs through engagement opportunities and then take action to enhance our Customer Service and the Customer Experience."[15] Commitment to this mission led to Southwest being ranked number one in customer satisfaction in 2011 by the US Department of Transportation.[16] Southwest averaged only 0.27 customer complaints per 100,000 customers boarded.[17]

Core Values—This is How We Do It

According to the Southwest web site, the company's core values are referred to as *The Southwest Way* and are broken down into the three categories shown below.[18] (It should be noted that all parenthetical comments for the remainder of this case study are those of the authors.)

Warrior Spirit (Fighting hard to be the best.)

- Work Hard (Southwest believes in the idea of working hard and playing hard. At Southwest, everyone is expected to work hard and everyone has the opportunity to play hard.)

- Desire to be the best (A company can only be the best if its employees believe in what the company does or stands for i.e., if they are able to satisfy their need for meaning or self-actualization by working there. Southwest employees strongly believe that what their company does—providing low fares so that average people can afford to fly— makes the world a better place. This means the work being done there is worth doing. Being the best also means winning lots of awards and designations and Southwest consistently wins a lot of them which makes its employees very proud to work there.)

- Be courageous (Act without fear when solving problems.)

- Display urgency (This shows the customer that you truly care.)

- Persevere (Don't give up.)

- Innovate (If the normal way of solving a problem doesn't work, invent a new way.)

A Servant's Heart (Putting others first.)

- Follow The Golden Rule (This tells employees to err on the side of doing the right thing. Southwest is not in the business of taking advantage of people.)

- Adhere to the Principles

- Treat others with respect

- Put others first (There's not room for selfish people at Southwest.)

- Be egalitarian (This means to treat everyone as an equal regardless of yours or the other person's position or title.)

- Demonstrate proactive Customer Service (Try to fix the problem before the customer has to ask you to fix it.)

- Embrace the SWA Family

    Fun-LUVing Attitude (Take your job seriously, but not yourself.)

- Have FUN (Smile and try to brighten the days of those around you.)

- Don't take yourself too seriously (Lighten up and enjoy the ride.)

- Maintain perspective (When solving problems, take into account what's really important and what isn't.)

- Celebrate successes (This recharges your batteries as well as the batteries of those around you.)

- Enjoy your work

- Be a passionate Teamplayer (Keep in mind that if the team succeeds, everyone succeeds.)

Within the context of its mission and core values, Southwest employees are free to exercise their autonomy and do their job as they see fit with no boss looking over their shoulder while they are doing work that they feel is worth doing.

As you can see, the culture at Southwest Airlines contains all four elements of a *full-engagement* culture. As such, the company provides its employees with the opportunity to experience satisfaction of all five need levels of the Maslow need hierarchy. This explains why Southwest has been profitable for 41 consecutive years.

Step Two: Hire Only Qualified People Who Mesh With the Culture

Like other companies with a high level of employee engagement, Southwest Airlines uses its mission and core values as the primary criteria for hiring new employees. Southwest firmly understands the reason for its success is the people who work there. As CEO Gary Kelly puts it, "Our people are our single greatest strength and most enduring long term competitive advantage."[19] Furthermore, as stated in the Southwest 2012 *One Report*, "Our people make Southwest Airlines one of the world's most admired companies."[20] This being the case, it's very important that Southwest bring people on board who have the right "attitude"—people who get excited about or find meaning in delivering the highest quality of Customer Service "with a sense of warmth, friendliness, individual pride, and Company Spirit." As former CEO Herb Kelleher once said, "We don't like to, but we will sacrifice expertise, education and experience to get a good attitude."[21] These are people who have a "Warrior Spirit," a "Servant's Heart," and a "Fun-LUVing Attitide." Comments made by employee Susan Bauer on the company web site epitomize the attitude that that Southwest is looking for: "It's incredible that we are given the opportunity to serve others on behalf of Southwest's noble cause: The opportunity to work with incredible and talented Coworkers, the opportunity to enjoy the best Leadership of any public company, and the opportunity to provide Positively Outrageous Customer Service every day out of LUV for our Customers and our Southwest Family."[22]

The way that Southwest screens for attitude is to conduct group interviews where the job candidate is asked questions and everyone is watching to see how he or she interacts with the other people in the room. The company feels this is a good indicator of how this individual will interact with customers while on the job. According to *Glassdoor.com*, job candidates are asked questions like the following: "How do you show your fun loving attitude at work?" "What was your most difficult customer care experience and how did you resolve it?" "Tell me about a time when you did something that was considered innovative at work." Or, "Talk about a time when you used humor in your work environment."[23] The goal is to hire only those people with a great sense of humor who are willing reach out to customers with a personality that stands out. This is what gives Southwest its unique competitive advantage. If this kind of work doesn't excite you, then you have no business applying for a job at Southwest.

The Hiring Process Must be Supported with a Relevant Training and/or Sponsorship Program that Teaches and Reinforces the Culture

Southwest has a Director of Onboarding and Leadership Development. This person is responsible for welcoming, mentoring and engaging new hires through their first year. This program helps every new recruit at Southwest embrace the principles of the company (including its culture) and successfully get their career off the ground at Southwest. One of the goals of the program is to show new employees how they fit into the "employee-centric" culture of a very large company. According to Cheryl Hughey, the Director of Onboarding and Leadership Development at Southwest, "The new hires need to know more about us from the moment they take the position. We need to be very clear upfront so they can learn about our culture and get a feel for who we are."[24] Commenting on how Southwest maintains a nurturing environment during a new employee's first six months at the company, Ms. Hughey had this to say: "You never get a second chance to make a first impression. We put a lot of effort into the new hires' first day at work. I hate to use the word "probation," but both the company and the employee are making decisions during the first six months. During the first period we offer continuous feedback. We also make sure to create clear expectations for their roles. We involve them in a variety of things in their work environment and we get new employees to participate in things the company is offering. We want to make sure they understand the medical and travel benefits and take advantage of them. Employees understand the freedom they have to make a positive experience and what that means. During the first six months we get them involved in going to spirit parties and our 'love at first bite' luncheon....We feel it's important to get new hires culturally acclimated. How do they understand the Southwest way (of doing things)?"[25]

Step Three: Leaders Must Lead, Not Give Orders

At Southwest Airlines, people who occupy what we would call "traditional management positions" are referred to as leaders. The reason is that's what they do; they lead, they don't give orders. As former CEO Herb Kelleher once said, "Southwest has the opposite of top-down management. The airline's headquarters is there to serve the line employees, not the other way around."[26] Employees are expected to exercise their freedom over their jobs and act in the best interest of the company and that means they get to decide what to do and how to do it. Leaders, on the other hand, serve as mentors, coaches, listeners and troubleshooters.

The leadership at Southwest also conducts an employee survey every two years to make sure its culture stays healthy. According to its 2012 *One Report,* "We conduct an Employee survey on a biennial basis, which allows us to take a collective picture of our entire workforce from several angles. These snapshots let us know how our Employees feel about working at Southwest. Employees' candid feedback is critical because it helps identify areas of strength at Southwest as well as areas where we have an opportunity to work together as a Team to improve.

In 2012, 55 percent of Southwest and AirTran Employees participated in the survey and provided feedback regarding their views of the Company. The survey, conducted by Mercer, evaluated 15 dimensions, and Employees were 70 percent or more favorable on 11 of the 15 dimensions.

The main objectives of the 2012 Employee survey were to gather Employee perceptions on a broad range of work, environment, and Cultural topics; assess and identify current levels of the components of Employee engagement and identify key drivers; and gather input on what it takes to be a best place to work. Southwest's scores on the engagement components are significantly above the norm on all benchmarked normative items, exceeding the norm by an average of 22 percentage points. All items in the Employee commitment dimension received ratings of at least 88 percent favorable, revealing a strong pride in the organization, connection to the organization's financial performance, and perception of Southwest as a desirable place to work. The most favorably rated item in the survey indicates that nearly all Employees (97 percent) are willing to "go the extra mile" to help serve Customers.

Our Leaders use this survey as a roadmap for improvement, creating action plans to address areas requiring attention and identifying overarching themes we can work on together. This feedback also helps us to make improvements on our journey to be a best place to work."[27]

CONCLUSION

It's very clear that the culture and leadership practices at Southwest Airlines fully embrace the Engagement Formula. This has resulted in Southwest earning a profit during the last 41 consecutive years—while its competitors have lost billions—and being an extremely desirable place to work.

ZAPPOS

Zappos is an online shoe and apparel shop currently based in Las Vegas, Nevada. The company was founded in 1999 by Nick Swinmurn after he couldn't find a pair of shoes that he wanted at his local mall. Later that year, Mr. Swinmurn approached Tony Hsieh and Alfred Lin with the idea of selling shoes online. According to Wikipedia, the company was originally lauched under the original domain name "ShoeSite.com." A few months after their launch, the company's name was changed from ShoeSite to Zappos (a variation of "zapatos," the Spanish word for "shoes") so as not to limit itself to selling only footwear. The company has experienced incredible growth and success going from minimal revenue in 1999 to $1billion in 2008. Today, Zappos is the largest online shoe store with 80 percent of its revenue coming from shoes and 20 percent coming from apparel. Because of its commitment to delivering the best possible customer service, Zappos has succeeded in cultivating a very loyal customer base with 75 percent of its sales coming from repeat buyers. In 2009, Zappos was bought by Amazon.com, but it continues to operate as an independent subsidary. Also, in 2009, Zappos cracked the *Fortune* List of 100 Best Companies To Work For and has made the list every year since.

Let's take a look at the leadership practices of Zappos and see how they match up with the Engagement Formula.

THE ENGAGEMENT FORMULA AT ZAPPOS

Step One: Create a Full-Engagement Culture that <u>Defines</u> the Organization and <u>Drives</u> Performance

A full-engagement culture has the following four elements:

Minimal Distractions—So Employees Can Focus on Performing Their Jobs

While Zappos is known for paying salaries that are competitive, but not industry leading, those salaries are still high enough to attract and retain their target employees—people who find meaning delivering WOW customer service over the phone in a call center. People are dying to come to work at Zappos. During 2013, Zappos received nearly 31,671 job applications for 167 open jobs[1] Money isn't the primary reason people want to work at Zappos; it's the culture. There is a very tight fit between Zappos employees and its quirky, wacky, wild and crazy, yet caring culture where everyone feels they're part of a huge, tightly knit family. For example, here are what a couple of Zappos employees had to say about its culture: "'I make half of what I made at my last job,' said Stephanie Simms, a buyer in the children's merchandising group. 'But it's not the money; it's the people. They are like family. We all come from so many different places that we spend Thanksgiving together.' She noted that despite a lack of college, she became a buyer in 18 months at Zappos. 'That could never happen at another company,' she said. Alesha Giles, a former Nordstrom employee from San Francisco, added that Zappos employees take care of one another. 'When I was going through chemotherapy, my coworkers drove me to get my treatments,' she said."[2]

Also, Zappos doesn't provide all the benefits that some of the other companies with a high level of employee engagement do. For example, it does not offer onsite day care, tuition reimbursement or 401(k) matching. This, however, doesn't seem to be an issue for Zappos employees. On the other hand, the benefits that Zappos does provide are excellent and, according to comments made on *Glassdoor.com*, employees are quite happy with them.[3] According to the Zappos web site those benefits include the following:[4]

Medical

Cigna OAP

Who's down with OPP? What the heck is OAP? It functions kind of like a PPO but is even better! That means an inexpensive plan where you don't need referrals! The Zappos Family covers 100% of the cost for your medical benefits and on average 85% of the cost for spouse, dependents, and partners. And, there is no pre-existing condition limitation!

Our plan covers acupuncture and prescriptions. And, the great news is that all preventative care will be covered at no charge.

Dental

Delta Dental PPO

Our dental plan covers 2 free exams per year and 3 free cleanings. You will have a $2000 plan maximum per year to cover basic and major services. We also provide an adult orthodontia benefit.

Vision

Superior Vision

Our vision plan provides you with a free eye exam and an allowance to cover frames/lenses or contacts.

Life Insurance

Hartford

The Zappos Family offers you life insurance and accident insurance. For both plans, your benefit is 1x your annual salary.

Other benefits

The Zappos Family is happy to also offer several other benefits. But for a preview, here's what else you can look forward to:

- Vacation

- Sick time

- Flexible Spending Account

- Onsite Wellness Services

- Employee Assistance Program

- Pet Insurance

- Pre-paid Legal

- 40% employee discount on the Zappos.com website

- Free breakfast, lunch, snacks, coffee, tea and more

- Paid volunteer time off

- Monthly Team Outings - to "Build a positive team and family environment"

- Access to 24 hour phones/internet during breaks/lunches

- Concierge Services available onsite

- Car Pool Program

- Nursing Room

- Bereavement Leave

- Several discounts with local businesses

- Nap rooms

Zappos also provides free lunches, no charge vending machines and has full-time in-house life coach on staff.[5]

For the individual who prefers a casual, laid-back work environment that rocks with fun and excitement, Zappos is the ideal place to work. The normal attire at Zappos is jeans, t-shirts and flip-flops. According to Wikipedia.org, "Each department has its own décor ranging from rainforest themed to Elvis themed and employees are encouraged to decorate their workspaces. For example, CEO Tony Hseih's desk, which sits in the middle of a cluster of cubicles, is decorated with vines and an inflatable monkey. Employees often lead spontaneous office parades which sometimes include cowbells, flags and costumes. In addition, managers are required to spend 10-20 percent of their working hours "goofing off" with employees outside of the office."[6] One employee on *Glassdoor.com described* the Zappos work environment as "the Disneyworld of offices."[7] Another employee had this to say about working at Zappos: "I have worked at Zappos for about three years now, and it has been the best three years of my life!

I have made some really great friends who I consider family. I wake up every day and look forward to going into the office, every day is a different day, you never know what's going to happen! I love the way the energy flows around the office; it definitely feeds from one person to the next!"[8]

Despite having to lay off eight percent of its workforce in November of 2008, the strong sense of family still permeates the Zappos workplace. The layoffs were forced by the economic downturn that occurred toward the end of that year. Zappos' major investor instructed Zappos to "cut expenses as much as possible and get to profitability and cash flow positive as soon as possible."[9] CEO Tony Hsieh decided to handle the matter openly and honestly. "Rather than try to spin the story as a 'strategic restructuring' as many other corporations were doing, we stuck by our core values and remained open and honest, not only with our employees, but with the press as well."[10] Instead of two weeks' severance or no severance as most companies were giving their laid off employees, Zappos paid each employee through the end of the year (about two months) and offered an additional amount to those who had been with Zappos for three years or more. Zappos also agreed to reimburse laid-off employees for up to six months of COBRA payments.[11] As Tony Hsieh put it, "We received a lot of media attention because we had been so public and transparent with our layoffs instead of trying to keep everything quiet. Going through such a dark period of time in the public eye really put our culture to the test. But as with all challenges, our employees figured out how to get through things and move on. Looking back now, I'm incredibly thankful and grateful that we all banded together and made sure that we didn't lose our team and family spirit. It really makes me feel proud of our employees. I also hope we never have to go through anything like that ever again."[12] This final statement means that layoffs at Zappos are an option only of last resort. Today, the jobs at Zappos are very secure. The company wouldn't have the high level of employee engagement that it enjoys nor would it have received nearly 31,671 job applications this past year if people felt otherwise.

From the above discussion, it's clear that the physiological and safety needs of Zappos employees are very well satisfied. This means that Zappos employee experience very few, if any distractions that would prevent them from giving all their attention and energy to performing their jobs.

Single Status—Everyone is an Equal

Zappos is known for its playful egalitarian culture. In addition, it has worked hard to blur the line between management and the rest of the employees. CEO Tony Hsieh and Fred Mossler (no title) don't like the term executive so the refer to themselves as the company's "monkeys."[13] Their desks are located in what is referred to as "Monkey Row." As Tony Hsieh says in his book, "At Zappos, we place a lot of emphasis on our culture because we are both a team and a family. We want to create an environment that is friendly, warm, and exciting. We encourage diversity in ideas, opinions and points of view....We believe that in general, the best ideas and decisions are made from the bottom up, meaning by those on the front lines that are closest to the issues and/or the customers. The role of the manager is to remove obstacles and enable his/her direct reports to succeed. This means that the best leaders are servant leaders. They serve those they lead."[14]

This means that at Zappos, employees are free to do their job as they see fit. In the call center, for example, employees do not have scripts, no one is looking over their shoulder and there is no limit on call times. The name of the game is simply to create a WOW experience for the customer. So far, the record for the longest call is around eight hours. Furthermore, if an employee comes up with an idea for something new, it's the manager's job to tell that person, "If you're passionate about it, run with it." [15]

From the above discussion, it's very clear that Zappos has a single-status culture.

Mission—This is What We Do

Zappos has aligned its entire organization around a single mission. That is: "To provide the best customer service possible."[16] It is the feeling at the company that this alignment around a single mission is what is responsible for its phenomenal growth.

Core Values—This is How We Do It

According to the company web site, Zappos has developed a set of ten core values to guide the day to day decisions and behavior of all Zappos employees in the execution of its mission. These core values are presented below with excerpted definitions of each core value taken from the Zappos web site:[17]

Deliver WOW Through Service

WOW is such a short, simple word, but it really encompasses a lot of things. To WOW, you must differentiate yourself, which means doing something a little unconventional and innovative. You must do something that's above and beyond what's expected.

Embrace and Drive Change

For some people, especially those who come from bigger companies, the constant change can be somewhat unsettling at first. If you are not prepared to deal with constant change, then you probably are not a good fit for the company.

Create Fun and A Little Weirdness

One of the things that makes Zappos different from a lot of other companies is that we value being fun and being a little weird. We don't want to become one of those big companies that feels corporate and boring. We want to be able to laugh at ourselves. We look for both fun and humor in our daily work.

Be Adventurous, Creative and Open-Minded

We do not want people to be afraid to take risks and make mistakes. We believe if people aren't making mistakes, then that means they're not taking enough risks. Over time, we want everyone to develop his/her gut about business decisions. We want people to develop and improve their decision-making skills. We encourage people to make mistakes as long as they learn from them.

Pursue Growth and Learning

It's important to constantly challenge and stretch yourself and not be stuck in a job where you don't feel like you are growing or learning.

Build Open and Honest Relationships With Communication

Strong, positive relationships that are open and honest are a big part of what differentiates Zappos from most other companies. Strong relationships allow us to accomplish much more than we would be able to otherwise.

Build a Positive Team and Family Spirit

We want to create an environment that is friendly, warm, and exciting. We encourage diversity in ideas, opinions, and points of view.

Do More With Less

While we may be casual in our interactions with each other, we are focused and serious about the operations of our business. We believe in working hard and putting in the extra effort to get things done.

Be Passionate and Determined

We are inspired because we believe in what we are doing and where we are going. We don't take "no" or "that'll never work" for an answer because if we had, then Zappos would have never started in the first place.

Be Humble

While we celebrate our individual and team successes, we are not arrogant nor do we treat others differently from how we would want to be treated. Instead, we carry ourselves with a quiet confidence because we believe that, in the long run, our character will speak for itself.

Within the context of its mission and core values, Zappos employees are free to do their jobs as they see fit. That means deciding what to do and how to do it without anyone looking over their shoulder.

How Zappos Developed Its Set of Core Values

It's important to note the process by which Zappos came up with these ten core values. At his previous company, Tone Hsieh was fed up with all the backstabbing and ladder climbing he saw. When he joined Zappos, he was determined that things would be different. One of the first things Mr. Hsieh did was ask the company's 300 employees to list the core values that the Zappos culture should be based upon. The initial list had 37 core values. During the course of a year, Mr. Hsieh emailed the entire company several times to get suggestions and feedback on which core values were most important to Zappos' employees. Like-minded suggestions were then grouped together until the exercise yielded the ten core values that continue to drive the company today which now has more than 1,400 employees.[18] According to Mr. Hsieh, "I was surprised the process took so long, but we wanted to make sure not to rush through the process because whatever core values we eventually came up with, we wanted to be ones that we could truly embrace. ...We wanted a list of committable core values that we were willing to hire and fire on. If we weren't willing to do that, then they weren't really 'values.'"[19]

Putting together a set of core values in this manner resulted in instant buy-in from the employees because they came up with them. From that point forward, only qualified prospective employees who mesh with these ten core values get hired.

As you can see, the culture at Zappos contains all four elements of a *full-engagement* culture. This means that Zappos provides its employees with the opportunity to satisfy all five levels of the Maslow need hierarchy. This is the reason behind Zappos phenomenal growth and why it is consistently ranked on the *Fortune* list of the Top100 Best Companies To Work For.

Step Two: Hire Only Qualified People Who Mesh With the Culture

Zappos is fanatic about making sure that new hires fit tightly with the Zappos culture. To illustrate, we went to the Zappos web site and downloaded a document titled *10 Tips to Make Sure That Your next New Hire Is A Culture Fit.*[20] Right after the download was completed, we received the following email from Zappos Insights:

"We hope that you have had a chance to download '10 Tips to Make Sure That Your next New Hire Is A Culture Fit.'

Our recruiting team worked diligently to create this resource and it has been very helpful for them in hiring the right people to be part of The Zappos Family. Of course by "right people" we mean those that are proficient in their specific job functions, as well as being a great fit within our company's culture.

Because we believe that our core values are a vital part of the health and well being of our company, we felt it necessary to make the Core Values a part of the hiring process. The tips we share on the sheet you downloaded is an example of how we have made that a reality. It is designed to catch the applicants off guard so that they do not give the standard canned responses associated with so many job interviews.

In order to accomplish our mission of 'delivering wow through service', it is imperative that we hire the right people. We need people that live and breathe The Zappos Family culture. It isn't about 'filling seats;' it is about finding the best individuals possible. We need a team of individuals that are committed to helping us reach our next level."[21]

The "Ten Tips" document from Zappos Insights describes the Zappos interview process as follows:[22]

How Many Interviews?

The qualified candidate can expect a three-stage process after applying for a position: a recruiting phone screen, a technical phone screen, and a 2-part onsite interview. These interviews and assessments allow the recruiter and hiring manager to be absolutely sure that the candidate has the skills needed to do the job, and is a culture fit for the team and company. Both aspects are important, and this is how the Zappos Family checks and rechecks for both:

The Recruiting Phone Screen

- 30 to 45 minutes

- Hosted by a recruiter

- Primary objective: basic core values match and to discuss any deal breakers: work history, career goals, salary requirements, and willingness to relocate.

- Secondary objective: has the applicant done their homework?
  ☐ Does applicant have a sense of what it is like to work with the Zappos Family?
  ☐ Does applicant want to work with the Zappos Family, or just want a job?

The Technical Phone Screen

- 30 to 45 minutes

- Hosted by the hiring manager

- Primary objective: assess technical fit at a high level

- Initial check for team and culture fit

Next Stop: Onsite Interview

If the applicant passes both phone screens (and, in some cases, a Skype interview with the department director, and/or additional members of the hiring manager's team), the recruiter will coordinate an onsite interview, which includes:

A Tour of the Zappos Family Offices

This is conducted by the recruiter or a member of the hiring manager's team. This is an opportunity for the candidate to get a sense of the physical environment, experience the culture a bit, and learn about the history of the Zappos Family, including current ventures and organizational structure. It's also a chance for the tour giver to gauge the applicant's reaction to what they are seeing. The Zappos Family is not for everyone. And the interviewers pay attention to the types of questions the applicant asks during the tour. Is there genuine interest and excitement about what the applicant seeing? Or are all the questions, 'me, me, me.'

Basic Skills Assessments

A recruiter will check for the skills relating to the position and to the call-center training program all new employees must complete: typing, grammar, and basic computer literacy.

Technical Interview

This is a 30-45 minute interview with the hiring manager and up to 6-8 other members of the team, in both one-on-one and group formats. The primary objective of these meetings is to get an in-depth assessment of the applicant's technical skills. Depending on the role, the candidate may also meet with stakeholders across departments as well.

Lunch with the Team

In order to get candidates out of the interview room and interacting a bit more comfortably, there is often a casual off-site interview. This gives the team a chance to see if there is a culture match with the group, and a chance for the hiring manager to make sure that the candidate can socialize outside of work.

Core Value Interview

This lasts another 45 to 60 minutes. The goal is to ensure that the candidate understands the culture, and has specific examples to share that support how they've already exhibited qualities that reflect our Core Values in previous positions. During the interview the job candidate is asked 2-5 questions regarding each of Zappos ten core values. These questions are contained in the *Zappos Family Core Values Interview Assessment Guide* which can be downloaded from *zapposinsights.com.*[23]

Zappos Insights then provides some crystal clear advice for making the final hiring decision: "**Moving forward in hiring a candidate has to be agreed upon by all interviewers. If all team members and the recruiter back that candidate, any seeds of doubt that could grow later on and negatively affect the new member or the team are minimized.**"[24]

For further information on how to recruit and hire for cultural fit, I recommend that you go to the Zappos Insights web site and download *10 Tips to Make Sure That Your next New Hire Is A Culture Fit.*[25]

The Hiring Process Must be Supported with a Relevant Training and/or Sponsorship Program that Teaches and Reinforces the Culture

At Zappos, once a prospective employee gets past the interview process, he or she must then go through the same four-week Customer Loyalty training program that call center employees are required to through. This is true for all new hires regardless of department or title. During this program, new hires absorb and begin to live the Zappos culture. This training also includes at least two weeks in the call center on the phone dealing with customers. Anyone who acts as though this type of work is beneath them is immediately shown the door. Also, in order to make sure that these new hires are truly embracing the Zappos culture, at the end of each week they are offered $2,000 on top of their current week's pay if they will agree to quit the company.[26] The goal is to weed out people who are not really committed to working at Zappos.

Step Three: Leaders Must Lead, Not Give Orders

At Zappos, leaders truly do lead, they don't give orders. As Tony Hsieh puts it in his book, "At Zappos, we place lot of emphasis on our culture because we are both a team and a family."[27] What this means is that when culture is emphasized there is no need for leaders to tell those around them what to do; they already know what to do because they understand the mission and core values of the company. Mr. Hsieh goes on to say, "We believe that in general, the best ideas and decisions are made from the bottom up, meaning by those on the front lines that are closest to the issues and/or the customers. The role of the manager is to remove obstacles and enable his/her direct reports to succeed. This means that the best leaders are servant leaders. They serve those they lead."[28]

Mr. Hsieh, also takes the pulse of Zappos' culture once a month with a *happiness survey*. Employees are asked if they agree or disagree with statements like the following:[29]

- I believe that the company has a higher purpose beyond just profits.

- My role at Zappos has a real purpose – it is more than just a job.

- I fell that I am in control of my career path and that I am progressing in my personal and professional development at Zappos.

- I consider my co-workers to be like my family and friends.

- I am very happy in my job.

Results of this survey are broken down by department and opportunities for improvement are identified and acted upon.[30] These actions make sure that the Zappos culture stays healthy

CONCLUSION

It's very clear that the culture and leadership practices at Zappos fully embrace all three steps of The Engagement Formula. This has not only made Zappos an extremely successful and highly admired company, but a very desirable place to work as well.

FRANK MYERS AUTO MAXX

Frank Myers Auto Maxx is a privately held used car dealership located in Winston-Salem, North Carolina. The used car industry has long suffered from a well-earned reputation for being unethical. We've all heard stories about used car dealerships taking advantage of their customers by selling them less than reliable vehicles, turning their back on them when they experience problems and repossessing their vehicles as soon as they miss a payment. For many of us, the expression "used car salesperson" conjures up images of a smiling salesperson eager to earn a commission, dressed in a loud sport coat, who slaps you on the back and says, "Have I got a deal for you!"

Frank Myers Auto Maxx is included as a case study to show how a business rooted in an industry with a much sullied reputation can get beyond that, have a highly engaged workforce and create a company that customers and potential employees flock to and competitors admire.

The original Frank Myers dealership was started in 1927 by Frank Myers. He was the Grandfather of the previous owner, Franklin Myers, and the Great-Grandfather of the current owner, Tracy Myers. Frank Myers Auto Maxx was recently recognized as the #1 Small Business in North Carolina by *Business Leader Magazine*, one of the Top 15 Independent Automotive Retailers in the United States by *Auto Dealer Monthly Magazine*, one of the Top 10 Internet Auto Retailers in the Nation, one of the Top 3 dealerships to work for in the country by *The Dealer Business Journal* and one of the fastest growing small businesses in America by *INC* magazine.[1] The company has 35 employees and its 2012 sales were $5.1 million. During the last three years its sales have grown by 35 percent.[2]

Let's take a look at the leadership practices at Frank Myers Auto Maxx and see how they match up with the Engagement Formula.

THE ENGAGEMENT FORMULA AT FRANK MYERS AUTO MAXX

Step One: Create a Full-Engagement Culture that <u>Defines</u> the Organization and <u>Drives</u> Performance

A full-engagement culture has the following four elements:

Minimal Distractions—So Employees Can Focus on Performing Their Jobs

The physiological and safety needs of the employees at Frank Myers Auto Maxx are fairly well satisfied. This wasn't always the case. Prior to 2005, salespeople were paid strictly on a commission basis which meant if they didn't sell anything, they didn't get paid. In addition, there was no health insurance or other benefits. As a result, turnover among the sales staff was high and morale was low because they didn't feel secure in their job. When current owner, Tracy Myers, purchased the dealership from his father in 2005, the first thing he did was put a non-commission pay plan in place for salespeople. Under this plan, salespeople are paid an above average salary like the rest of the employees at the dealership plus a bonus that is tied to the achievement of overall company goals rather than just the number of cars sold.[3] Employees are also provided with an excellent benefit package that includes health insurance, a five-day work week and annual tenure bonuses (based on the number of years worked at the dealership) that can be taken in the form of cash or paid time off.

As a result of implementing this non-commission pay plan, turnover among salespeople became almost nonexistent overnight.[4] Competition among salespeople was replaced with team work and a family atmosphere. In addition, emphasis among sales people shifted from selling cars to helping customers solve problems—namely helping them "find, qualify for and own the vehicle of their dreams with little or no money down...even with less than perfect credit." This arrangement has enabled salespeople at Frank Myers Auto Maxx to spend more time with customers and keep costs down at the same time.[5]

In order to remove further distractions from its Non-Commissioned Sales Team, the company built a Business Development Center in 2009 to handle all incoming and outgoing calls and emails, incoming and outgoing customer service calls and administrative duties. This allows the Sales Team to focus 100 percent of their time and effort on the customer and the Frank Myers Auto Maxx way of doing business.[6]

The work environment at Frank Myers Auto Maxx reflects the flair of its owner. It's very much a party atmosphere because the philosophy at this dealership is that buying a car should be fun. This atmosphere includes loud music, bright colors, costumed characters wandering around, people wearing funny hats who are high-fiving each other and dancing around and bi-annual community picnics with free food. Frank Myers Auto Maxx is also known for putting the customer "on stage." For example, customers who purchase a car get to walk up a red carpet and bang a gong as they are applauded by employees and anyone else who happens to in the area and welcomed to the Frank Myers family. These episodes are videoed and placed on the Frank Myers web site as well as YouTube. This is all done in the interest of making the process of buying a car fun and customers love it.

As Tracy Myers puts it, "We're not for everybody...We have a good time. Some people don't like buying a car in an atmosphere like this and that's okay. But there's a lot of love here and you can feel it when you walk through the door."[7]

By replacing its commission pay plan with a non-commission play plan that includes an above average salary and benefits, creating a family environment where jobs are secure and a party atmosphere where work is fun, Frank Myers Auto Maxx has succeeded in removing most, if not all, of the day to day distractions that would prevent its employees from giving all their energy and attention to performing their job.

Single Status—Everyone is an Equal

The culture of Frank Myers Auto Maxx reflects the values of its owner Tracy Myers. He's humble, personable and cares about his employees as well as his customers. Furthermore, he's all about love and believes employees and customers ought to be treated as family members—equals. This means employees have the autonomy to work on their own terms and do their job as they see fit. This is why they are able to maintain such a festive party atmosphere at Frank Myers Auto Maxx that never goes stale.

Mission—This is What We Do

Frank Myers Auto Maxx has aligned its organization around a mission with two levels. The first level is the overall **Team Mission** which is: "to improve the public opinion of auto dealership employees, to help Frank Myers Auto Maxx Team Members achieve a life that's ESP-Enjoyable, Simple & Prosperous and to enable good people to get the transportation they want and need."

The second level is the **Individual Team Member Mission** which is: "To specialize in helping people find, qualify for and own the vehicle of their dreams with little or no money down...even with less than perfect credit."[8]

Core Values—This is How We Do It

Frank Myers Auto Maxx has developed a set of five core values that guide the day to day decisions and behavior of its employees in the execution of its mission. These core values have been excerpted from the company web site and are presented below.[9]

Working at Frank Myers Auto Maxx (FMAM) should be fun

Team Members understand that life is too short not to have fun. This is why they try to find enjoyment in everything they do at FMAM.

FMAM Team Members are seen as trusted friends rather than salespeople

FMAM Team Members are on the side of the consumer as opposed to being a salesperson who is looking out only for themselves and the dealership.

FMAM wants to be in a class of its own

FMAM doesn't want to compete with other dealerships; it wants to set itself apart and be in a class of its own. This is why FMAM takes its Team Members out of the commodity game (where low price is the only thing that matters) and positions them as industry experts who work side-by-side with customers to solve their problems and help them get the car they want.

FMAM Team Members are rewarded for the value they provide their customers, not just for selling cars

FMAM positions its Team Members to deliver tremendous value to their customers and they are rewarded handsomely in exchange.

FMAM Team Members are expected to make a positive impact on the communities they serve

FMAM Team Members should be influential members of their community and help create its future.

Within the context of its mission and core values, the employees of Frank Myers Auto Maxx are free to exercise their autonomy and do their job as they see fit. That means deciding what to do and how to do it without a boss looking over their shoulder.

As you can see, the culture at Frank Myers Auto Maxx contains all four elements of a *full-engagement* culture. This means that the company provides its employees with the opportunity to experience the satisfaction of all five levels of the Maslow need hierarchy. This is why it was able to become the #1 Small Business in North Carolina and one of the top three dealerships to work for in the United States.

Step Two: Hire Only Qualified People Who Mesh With the Culture

Like other companies with a high level of employee engagement, Frank Myers Auto Maxx uses its culture as the primary criterion for hiring new employees. The leadership at Frank Myers Auto Maxx understands that the success of the dealership is the result of having employees who are engaged with their work. They also understand that this can only occur if there is a tight fit between what employees feel is worthwhile work and the work opportunities that are available at Frank Myers Auto Maxx.

According to an article by Frank Ziegler, which appeared in autodealer.com, "Frank Myers Auto Maxx maintains their high standard of excellence by staffing their team with people who have a great attitude, an outgoing personality, and eagerness to learn."[10] According to owner, Tracy Myers, things work at our dealership because, "...we hire the right type of person—we don't look for a cowboy who wants to do it his own way. The result is very low turnover and surprisingly low costs. As a customer focused company, I can see my cost of sales, as compared with other dealers, and we're in the lower half."[11] In other words, Frank Myers Auto Maxx is very particular about making sure it hires only those people who mesh with the company's mission and core values.

The Hiring Process Must be Supported with a Relevant Training and/or Sponsorship Program that Teaches and Reinforces the Culture

New employees at Frank Myers Auto Maxx go through a 30 day paid training/orientation program before they can even begin working with a guest (customer) other than saying hello. The purpose of this program is to welcome the new hires into the Frank Myers Auto Maxx family, teach them the company culture and show them how to succeed within it. These new hires are referred to as "Green Peas." Upon completing the training program the new hires stay with a mentor for an additional 60 days. The job of the mentor is to serve as role model, coach and sounding board. At the end of the 60 days, mentors are rewarded for their efforts. They can take this reward either in the form of cash or paid time off.[12]

Step Three: Leaders Must Lead, Not Give Orders

On its web site, Frank Myers Auto Maxx promises prospective employees a great work environment and a chance to set themselves apart from the routine of the average job.[13] The company more than delivers on that promise, because working at this dealership is anything but ordinary. It's about customers and employees coming together as a family that truly cares about each other. Every day, work involves a festive party atmosphere with lots of over the top antics in an environment that's couched in love and respect. Such an environment could not be created or maintained if bosses were telling subordinates what to do and how to do it. This is why at Frank Myers Auto Maxx, leaders assume the role coach or mentor rather than that of a traditional manager.

CONCLUSION

It's very clear that the culture and leadership practices of Frank Myers Auto Maxx fully embrace the Engagement Formula. Doing so has enabled this dealership to move way beyond the negative image that is so often associated with the used car industry and become a dealership that customers and potential employees flock to and competitors admire.

PART FIVE - IMPLEMENTATION:

A PLANNING GUIDE FOR IMPLEMENTING THE ENGAGEMENT FORMULA IN YOUR ORGANIZATION

IMPLEMENTATION PLANNING GUIDE

Note 1: This *Implementation Planning Guide* is annotated in that it provides lots of explanation as to how to execute each part of the implementation process. The goal is to save you the trouble and bother of having to go back to the main text of this book and looking up this information.

Note 2: This *Implementation Planning Guide* is also available as a free 8.5 x 11 inch download from my website at www.RossReck.com/downloads.

Step One: Create a Full-Engagement Culture that <u>Defines</u> Your Organization and <u>Drives</u> Performance

- **Minimal Distractions—So Employees Can Focus on Performing Their Jobs.** If employees' physiological and safety needs are not fairly well satisfied, this creates distractions which means employees can't give their full energy and attention to performing their jobs. This is why organizations with a high level of employee engagement offer compensation packages that are at or above industry levels, provide fairly generous benefit packages, a job that is reasonably secure and a work environment that's pleasant and safe. They want to remove as many distractions as possible so their employees can focus on doing their best work.

  o **Compensation**—Employees can't become engaged with their work if they think they're unfairly paid or they're not making enough money to support themselves.

1. What is your plan to make sure that employee compensation is fair and equitable?

2. Are you going to use the compensation levels of other organizations in your area or industry as benchmarks to make sure the compensation levels at your company are competitive? If so, which organizations and who is going to do the benchmarking?

3. Are you going to compare market data to the job titles at your organization to make sure that employee compensation is fair and equitable? If so, what market data are you going to use?

4. Are you going to include bonuses and/or profit sharing in your

compensation? If so, how will they be determined and distributed?

○ **Benefits**—Remember, the benefits that your organization offers reflect how much it values its employees. Once again, the goal is to minimize the day to day distractions so that employees can focus all their energy and attention on their jobs.

1. Are you going to use the benefit offerings of other organizations in your area or industry as benchmarks to make sure the benefit offerings at your organization are competitive? If so, which organizations and who is going to do the benchmarking?

2. It's important to gather input from employees to find out what benefits are important to them. How do you plan to do this? (Interviews email questionnaires, meetings with employee groups, etc.)

- **Work Environment**—It should be pleasant and conducive to teamwork and innovation. The work environment also reflects how much your organization values its employees.

    1. How to you plan to solicit input from your employees regarding how the physical work environment can be made more pleasant (more appealing colors, more windows, better lighting, etc.) and what amenities(break rooms, vending machines, onsite day care, workout room, etc.) they would they like to see added? (Interviews, email questionnaires, meetings with employee groups, etc.)

- **Job Security**—Employees <u>can't</u> become engaged with their work if their future at the company is uncertain. Layoffs should only be used as the last resort when it comes to dealing with economic downturns. Your policy regarding layoffs also reflects how much your company values its employees.

    1. How do you plan to communicate to your employees that their jobs are fairly well secure? (Adopt some kind of no-layoff policy—maybe a policy where instead of laying people off, everyone

takes a pay cut of a certain amount or gets their hours cut by a certain percentage during a business downturn.)

2. How do you plan to solicit employee input on this matter? If employees have a hand in determining the policy, they'll support it when a downturn comes.

- **Single-Status—Everyone is an Equal**. Remember, equality means autonomy—the the freedom to question, the freedom to challenge and the freedom for employees to be themselves, have fun and do their jobs as they see fit. Autonomy is critical because without it, employees cannot pursue satisfaction of their esteem needs which is a very powerful source of motivation.

    1. What changes need to be made in your organization to ensure everyone is treated with the utmost dignity and respect?

2. What symbols of unequal status need to be done away with? (Things like separate parking lots, separate dining rooms, time clocks for some employees and not others, special parking spaces for "important people" and so forth.)

3. What "us versus them" attitudes and practices need to changed?

4. What changes do you need to make in the way you share information? (Information must be shared with everyone at once rather than going to the "important" people first and eventually filtering down to the less important people.)

5. To communicate equality and a strong sense of belonging, you might consider adopting a special name for fellow employees as many companies with a high level of engagement have done

such as "family members." "associates," "Googlers," "Dreamworkers," or "Zapponians."

- **Mission—This is What We Do.** This is a brief statement of what your organization does or stands for. For example, the mission Zappos is to "provide the best customer service possible" while the mission of JetBlue is "bringing humanity back to air travel." In order to be effective, your mission must be understood and embraced by all employees.

  1. Does your organization currently have a mission that is understood and embraced by all employees?

  2. If not, you need to start from scratch and create a mission that's relevant to what your organization does or stands for. If this is the case, how do you plan to involve all of your employees in the creation of your mission? (Keep in mind that if your employees aren't actively involved in the process of creating your mission, chances are they won't embrace it.)

- **Core values—This is How We Do It.** Core values communicate how the employees within an organization are going to go about the business of executing its mission. For example, the mission at Zappos is to provide the best customer service possible. They have developed the following set of ten core values that define how the company will go about executing its mission:

  o   Deliver WOW Through Service

  o   Embrace and Drive Change

  o   Create Fun and A Little Weirdness

  o   Be Adventurous, Creative and Open-Minded

  o   Pursue Growth and Learning

  o   Build Open and Honest Relationships With Communication

  o   Build a Positive Team and Family Spirit

  o   Do More With Less

  o   Be Passionate and Determined

  o   Be Humble

These ten core values represent behavioral expectations for Zappos employees and, in doing so they direct their efforts toward the goals of the organization. For example, "Deliver WOW Through Service," tells employees that pleasing the customer is not enough. Zappos employees are expected to blow the customers' socks off. This means continually coming up with new and innovative ways of doing so. "Create Fun and A Little Weirdness" tells employees that they are free to be themselves and have fun while doing their jobs. "Be Humble" communicates clearly that arrogant, condescending and mean spirited behavior is not tolerated at Zappos. Within the context of these core values then, Zappos employees are free to exercise their autonomy to do their job as they see fit. Nobody is there to look over their shoulders.

It's important to note the way that Zappos went about figuring out its core values because their process produces instant buy-in. CEO TonyHsieh asked each of the company's 300 employees at the time to list the core values that the Zappos culture should be based upon. The initial list had 37 core values. During the course of a year, Mr. Hsieh emailed the entire company several times to get suggestions and feedback on which core values were most important to Zappos' employees. Like-minded suggestions were then grouped together until the exercise yielded the ten core values that continue to drive the company today which now has more than 1,800 employees. According to Mr. Hsieh, "I was surprised the process took so long, but we wanted to make sure not to rush through the process because whatever core values we eventually came up with, we wanted to be ones that we could truly embrace. ...We wanted a list of committable core values that we were willing to hire and fire on. If we weren't willing to do that, then they weren't really 'values.'"

Putting together a set of core values in this manner resulted in instant buy-in from the employees because they came up with them. From that point forward, only qualified prospective employees who mesh with these ten core values get hired.

1. What is your plan to involve all of your organization's employees in developing a list of core values?

Step Two: Hire Only Qualified People Who Mesh With the Culture

Hiring people under *The Engagement Formula* leadership model is not about "filling seats" or hiring based on a resume, it's about finding qualified people who mesh tightly with your culture. This is why organizations with a high level of employee engagement use their culture (mission and core values) as the primary criterion for hiring new employees.

1. Develop a hiring process that will ensure that your new hires are both technically qualified and mesh tightly with your culture. I suggest you go to zapposinsights.com and download the following two documents:

    • *Tips to Make Sure That Your next New Hire Is A Culture Fit*
    • *Zappos Family Core Values Interview Assessment Guide*

    These two documents will provide you with an incredible amount of insight regarding how to put your own hiring process together that will ensure that you hire only qualified people who fit tightly with your culture.

The Hiring Process Must be Supported with a Relevant Training and/or Sponsorship Program that Teaches and Reinforces the Culture.

1. Develop a training and/or sponsorship program that will ensure that all new hires quickly absorb and begin to live all the core values of your company.

Step Three: Leaders Must Lead, Not Give Orders

In a high engagement organization, there is no need for leaders to tell their followers what to do and how to do it—they already know this from their organization's mission and core values. Instead the role of a leader is to do whatever it takes to enable his or her followers to do an excellent job. Examples of what leaders do in high-engagement organizations are presented below.

- **Leaders Set the Example.** In a high-engagement culture, leaders set the example when it comes to treating everyone as equals and living the organization's core values. For example, Herb

166 100% Employee Engagement - <u>Guaranteed</u>!

Kelleher, former CEO of Southwest Airlines set the standard when it came to living his organization's core values. It was not uncommon for him to show at an airport, after midnight, dressed in a set of coveralls and carrying a box of doughnuts to help the cleaning crews clean planes. This sent a very clear message that just because he was the CEO, it didn't mean he was above doing the dirty work required to make an airline successful.

1. What are some things that the leaders at your organization can do to set the example when it comes to treating everyone as equals and living the core values of your company?

- **Leaders Provide Support.** Leaders ask questions, listen and remove barriers and obstacles. In other words, their job is to do whatever it takes to enable the people around them to do an outstanding job. No job is too menial if it enables another employee to do an excellent job. For example, in addition to helping flight attendants pick up trash in the plane during quick turnarounds, the pilots at Southwest Airlines also help gate agents push wheel chair passengers on to the plane so that Southwest can make an on-time departure.

1. What are some things that the leaders at your organization can do to provide support to those around them?

- **Leaders Make Sure the Culture Stays Healthy.** For example, CEO, Tony Hsieh, checks on the health of Zappos culture once a month with a *happiness survey*. Employees are asked if they agree or disagree with statements like the following:

    o I believe that the company has a higher purpose beyond just profits.

    o My role at Zappos has a real purpose – it is more than just a job.

    o I feel that I am in control of my career path and that I am progressing in my personal and professional development at Zappos.

    o I consider my co-workers to be like my family and friends.

    o I am very happy in my job.

    Results of this survey are broken down by department and opportunities for improvement are identified and acted upon.

    1. Develop a plan to set up a cultural oversight group or committee whose

purpose is to make sure your organization's culture is healthy and functioning. This group should be made up of employees from all levels of your organization.

2. How often will this group meet?

3. How will this group check on the health of your organization's culture (Interviews with employees, email surveys, meeting with employee groups, etc.)?

4. How often will this group check on the health of your organization's culture?

5. What will be done with the information that is gathered?

NOTES AND OTHER INFORMATION

NOTES

_____

INTRODUCTION

1 John Brooks, *Business Adventures* (New York: Open Road Media; reprint edition, 2014).

2 "Table: Xerox' History: Highs and Lows," *BloombergBusinessweek Magazine,* (March 4, 2001), http://www.businessweek.com/stories/2001-03-04/table-xerox-history-the-highs-and-lows, (accessed on August, 27, 2014).

3 Devon-Ritchie, "A Live Television Demonstration Makes the Xerox 914 the First Successful Photocopier," *Famous Daily,* (September 16, 2012), http://famousdaily.com/history/first-photocopier-xerox-914.html, (accessed on August 27, 2014).

4 Brooks, *Business Adventures, 193.*

5 Ibid.

6 Steve Crabtree, "Worldwide, 13% of Employees are Engaged at Work," *GALLUP World* (October 8, 2013), http://www.gallup.com/poll/165269/worldwide-employees-engaged-work.aspx (accessed on May 9, 2014),

7 . Douglas McGregor, *The Human Side of Enterprise: 25th Anniversary Printing* (New York: McGraw-Hill, 1985), 4.

8 Ibid., 42.

9 Ibid., 49.

CHAPTER 1: UNDERSTANDING HUMAN MOTIVATION IS THE KEY TO SOLVING THE EMPLOYEE ENGAGEMENT PROBLEM

[1] McGregor, *The Human Side of Enterprise*, 36.

[2] A. H. Maslow, "A Theory of Human Motivation," *Psychological Review* 50 (1943): 370-396, http://psychclassics.yorku.ca/Maslow/motivation.htm: 13 of 17.

[3] Ibid., 3.

[4] SAS, Employee Culture. http://www.sas.com/company/csr/employees.html (accessed January 10, 2012).

[5] Google, Benefits. http://www.google.com/intl/en/jobs/lifeatgoogle/benefits/index.html (accessed January 11, 2012).

[6] Gary Hamel, *W. L. Gore: Lessons from a Management Revolutionary* (March 18, 2010) http://blogs.wsj.com/management/2010/03/18/wl-gore-lessons-from-a-management-revolutionary/ (accessed November 15, 2011): 2 of 4.

[7] David Keonig, "Southwest Airlines Co-Founder Herb Kelleher Opens Up About Industry, *Tulsa World* (July 3, 2011) http://www.tulsaworld.com/business/article.aspx?subjectid=45&articleid=20110703_45_E2_CUTLIN65052 (accessed November 10, 2011).

[8] *The Washington Post,* "On Leadership: Google CEO Eric Schmidt on Workplace Culture," video, 7:27, http://www.washingtonpost.com/national/on-leadership-google-ceo-eric-schmidt-on-workplace-

culture/2011/07/15/gIQAajkPGI_video.html (accessed on October 10, 2011).

9 Maslow, "A Theory of Motivation," 7.

10 HRM Session 8: *Reward Systems—An Alternative View,* Case: SAS Institute, http://www.google.com/#hl=en&sugexp=pfwl&xhr=t&q=HRM+Sess ion+8%3A+Reward+systems-- an+alternative+view+Case%3A+SAS+Institute&cp=70&pf=p&sclient =psy- ab&source=hp&aq=f&aqi=&aql=&oq=HRM+Session+8:+Reward+syst ems-- an+alternative+view+Case:+SAS+Institute&pbx=1&bav=on.2,or.r_gc. r_pw.,cf.osb&fp=90c1eb6c7005c121&biw=1408&bih=775, 3 (accessed October 8, 2011).

11 Gary Hamel, *The Future of Management* (Boston: Harvard Business School Press, 2007), 92.

12 Maslow, "A Theory of Motivation," 7.

13 Abraham H. Maslow, *Maslow on Management* (New York: John Wiley & Sons, Inc., 1998), 16.

14 Maslow, *Maslow on Management,* 1.

15 Frederick Herzberg, Bernard Mausner and Barbara Bloch Snyderman, *The Motivation to Work* (New York: John Wiley & Sons, Inc., 1959), 114-115.

16 McGregor, *The Human Side of Enterprise,* 55.

17 Maslow, *Maslow on Management,*14.

18 Ibid., 9-10.

[19] Zappos.com, Inc., *2010 Culture Book* (available free from Zappos Insights-- http://www.zapposinsights.com/culture-book), 55.

[20] Douglas McGregor, *The Professional Manager* (New York: McGraw-Hill, 1967), 10-11.

[21] HRM Session 8: *Reward Systems—An Alternative View*, 3.

[22] Lucien Rhodes, "The Un-Manager," *Inc.* (August 1,1982), 1 www.google.com/#hl=en&sugexp=pfwl&xhr=t&q=Bill+Gore+and+Jack+Doughtery&cp=28&pf=p&sclient=psy-ab&source=hp&aq=f&aqi=&aql=&oq=Bill+Gore+and+Jack+Doughtery&pbx=1&bav=on.2,or.r gc.r pw.,cf.osb&fp=90c1eb6c7005c121&biw=1408&bih=775 (Accessed on January 21, 2012).

[23] Zappos, Inc., *2010 Culture Book,* 208.

[24] Amy Lyman, "NetApp-Culture-Values-Leadership #1 on the 2009 list of the 100 best companies to Work For," *Great Place to Work Institute* (2009), 2 http://www.google.com/#hl=en&sugexp=pfwl&xhr=t&q=Great+places+to+work+institute+netapp+2009&cp=42&pf=p&sclient=psy-ab&source=hp&aq=f&aqi=&aql=&oq=Great+places+to+work+institute+netapp+2009&pbx=1&bav=on.2,or.r gc.r pw.,cf.osb&fp=90c1eb6c7005c121&biw=1408&bih=775 (accessed on January 21, 2012).

CHAPTER 2: THE TRADITIONAL MANAGEMENT MODEL AND WHY IT PREVENTS EMPLOYEES FROM BECOMING ENGAGED WITH THEIR WORK

[1] McGregor, *The Human Side of Enterprise,* 33-34.

[2] McGregor, *The Human Side of Enterprise,* 77.

CHAPTER 3: CREATING A NEW MODEL THAT CAUSES EMPLOYEES TO BECOME ENGAGED WITH THEIR WORK

[1] Southwest Airlines, Our Benefits. http://www.southwest.com/html/about-southwest/careers/benefits.html (access January 23, 2012)

[2] David Koenig, "Southwest Airlines Co-Founder Herb Kelleher Opens Up About Industry."

[3] Southwest Airlines, "We're All in This Together," YouTube Video, 7:34, http://www.youtube.com/watch?v=3RI08CwiLjw (accessed January 23, 2012).

[4] Annette Dalla, "Herb Kelleher Discusses the importance of Culture at VIP Speaker Series," *McCombs Today,* (February 12, 2009) http://mccombstoday.org/2009/02/herb-kelleher-discusses-importance-of-culture-at-vip-speaker-series (accessed January 22, 2012).

[5] Herb Kelleher, "A Culture of Commitment," *Leader to Leader* No.4, (Spring, 1997): 2, http://www.google.com/#sclient=psy-ab&hl=en&source=hp&q=a+culture+of+commitment+herb+kelleher&aq=0&aqi=g1g-v2&aql=&oq=&pbx=1&bav=on.2,or.r gc.r pw.,cf.osb&fp=90c1eb6c7005c121&biw=1408&bih=775 (accessed on January 23, 2012).

[6] SAS, Newsroom/Press Releases, http://www.sas.com/news/preleases/great-workplace-US-Fortune-2013.html (accessed July 24, 2013).

[7] SAS, Company/Corporate Responsibility. http://www.sas.com/company/csr/employees.html (accessed January 22, 2012).

[8] Amy Lyman, "SAS Institute: 2010 #1 Company to Work for in America," *Great Place to Work Institute, Inc.,* (2010), 4

http://www.google.com/url?sa=t&rct=j&q=sas%20institute%20%2
02010%20%231%20company%20to%20work%20for%20in%20a
merica&source=web&cd=1&sqi=2&ved=0CCwQFjAA&url=http%3A
%2F%2Fresources.greatplacetowork.com%2Farticle%2Fpdf%2Fsas
_2010.pdf&ei=zJEdT_HqDuWq2QXqwqWEDA&usg=AFQjCNGQnuDch
nx-q6CEu4_s1ibnufl8Vg (accessed on January 23, 2012).

⁹ Google, The Google Culture.
http://www.google.com/about/corporate/company/culture.html
(accessed on Jauary 23, 2012).

¹⁰ Tony Hsieh, *Delivering Happiness: A Path to Profits, Passion and Purpose* (New York: Business Plus, 2010), 154.

¹¹ Ibid., 184.

¹² Ibid., 155-157.

¹³ Ibid., 157.

¹⁴ Greg Bensinger, "Amazon's Current Employees Raise the Bar for New Hires," *The Wall Street Journal Online,* (January 7, 2014). http://www.wsj.com/articles/SB1000142405270230475350457928
5133045398344 (accessed on January 8, 2014).

¹⁵ Dick Richards, "At Zappos Culture Pays," *Culture +Business* (August 24, 2010), 1 http://www.strategy-business.com/article/10311?gko=c784e (accessed on January 23, 2012).

¹⁶ Adam Bryant, "On a Scale of 1 to10, How Weird are You?" *New York Times Business Day.* (January 9, 2010) http://www.nytimes.com/2010/01/10/business/10corner.html?pa
gewanted=all (accessed on January 23, 2012).

¹⁷ Ibid.

[18] NetApp, Careers/Frequently Asked Questions. http://www.netapp.com/us/careers/find-job/faqs.html (accessed on January 23, 2012).

[19] Southwest Airlines, Fact Sheet/Fun Facts. http://www.swamedia.com/channels/Corporate-Fact-Sheet/pages/corporate-fact-sheet (accessed on May 12, 2014).

[20] Dawn Gilbertson, "Kelleher Entertains, Enlightens at Award Ceremony," *The Arizona Republic,* (December 9, 2005) http://www.flyertalk.com/forum/southwest-rapid-rewards/502002-herb-kelleher-entertains-enlightens-award-ceremony.html (accessed on January 24, 2012).

[21] W. L. Gore & Associates, Inc., Tips for Your Career Search at Gore/Interview Teams. http://www.gore.com/en_xx/careers/professionals/tips/job-hunting-tips.html (accessed on January 24, 20112).

[22] Joseph Walker, "Google: Obsessed With its Employees," *FINS Technology—Tech Job Watch* (May 11, 2011) http://it-jobs.fins.com/Articles/SB130505696841014767/Google-Obsessed-With-Its-Employees (accessed on January 24, 2012).

[23] W. L. Gore & Associates, Inc., Who We Are/Working in Our Unique Culture/Sponsors. http://www.gore.com/en_xx/careers/whoweare/ourculture/gore-company-culture.html (accessed on January 24, 2012).

[24] Richards, "At Zappos, Culture Pays," 2.

[25] Hsieh, *Delivering Happiness,* 158.

[26] Gary Hamel, "W. L. Gore: Lessons from a Management Revolutionary," *The Wall Street Journal* (March 18, 2010), 4 http://blogs.wsj.com/management/2010/03/18/wl-gore-lessons-from-a-management-revolutionary/ (accessed on May 12, 2014).

27 Richards, "At Zappos, Culture Pays," 3.

28 Hsieh, *Delivering Happiness,* 150.

29 Conversation with Harry Paul, coauthor of *Fish! A Remarkable Way to Boost Morale and Improve Results* (New York: Hyperion, 2000), January 20, 2012.

30 Charles S. Jacobs, *Management Rewired* (New York: Portfolio—published by the Penguin Group, 2009), 88.

31 Ibid.

32 Ibid., 89.

33 Ibid.

CASE STUDIES: W. L. GORE & ASSOCIATES

1 Alan Deutchman, " The Fabric of Creativity," *Fast Company.com*, (December 19, 2007), 2 http://www.fastcompany.com/magazine/89/open_gore.html (accessed on February 1, 2012),

2 Ibid.

3 W. L. Gore & Associates, Inc., What We Offer/Compensation. http://www.gore.com/en_xx/careers/whatweoffer/compensation/compensation.html (accessed on February 1, 2012).

4 Ibid., What We offer/Our Commitment to Gore Associates. http://www.gore.com/en_xx/careers/whatweoffer/gore-opportunities.html (accessed on February 15, 2012).

5 Ibid., What We Offer/Benefits. http://www.gore.com/en_xx/careers/whatweoffer/benefits/benefits.html (accessed on February 1, 2012).

[6] "100 Best Companies to Work For," *CNNMoney* (2011) http://money.cnn.com/magazines/fortune/bestcompanies/2011/snapshots/31.html (accessed on February 1, 2012).

[7] Amy Lyman, "Gore—Success With Simplicity," *Great Place to Work Institute, Inc.,* (2009), 1 www.executivemanagementskills.com/pdf/WLGore.pdf (accessed on February 2012).

[8] Ibid., 4.

[9] W. L. Gore & Associates, Inc., Our Culture/A Team-Based, Flat Lattice Organization. http://www.gore.com/en_xx/aboutus/culture/index.html (accessed on February 1, 2012).

[10] W. L. Gore & Associates, Inc., Who We Are/Working in Our Unique Culture. http://www.gore.com/en_xx/careers/whoweare/ourculture/gore-company-culture.html (accessed on February 1, 1012).

[11] Hamel, "W. L. Gore: Lessons from a Management Revolutionary," 3.

[12] W. L. Gore & Associates, Inc., Who We Are/Working in Our Unique Culture. http://www.gore.com/en_xx/careers/whoweare/ourculture/gore-company-culture.html (Accessed on February 1, 2012).

[13] Ibid., About Gore. http://www.gore.com/en_xx/aboutus/ (accessed on February 1, 2012).

[14] Ibid, Who We Are/What We Believe. http://www.gore.com/en_xx/careers/whoweare/whatwebelieve/gore-culture.html (accessed on February 1, 2012).

[15] Ibid.

[16] Lyman, "Gore—Success with Simplicity," 1.

¹⁷ W. L. Gore & Associates, Inc., Who We Are/Is Gore a Good Fit for You?
http://www.gore.com/en xx/careers/whoweare/rightforyou/working-at-gore.html (accessed on February 1, 2012).

¹⁸ Lyman, "Gore—Success with Simplicity," 1-2.

¹⁹ W. L. Gore & Associates, Inc., Who We Are/Working in Our Unique Culture.
http://www.gore.com/en xx/careers/whoweare/ourculture/gore-company-culture.html (accessed on February 1, 2012).

²⁰ Gary Hamel, "W. L. Gore: Lessons from a Management Revolutionary, Part 2," *The Wall Street Journal* (April 2, 2010), 1
http://blogs.wsj.com/management/2010/04/02/wl-gore-lessons-from-a-management-revolutionary-part-2/ (accessed on February 1, 2012).

²¹ Hamel, "W. L. Gore: Lessons from a Management Revolutionary," 3-4.

²² Hamel, "W. L. Gore: Lessons from a Management Revolutionary, Part 2," 3.

²³ Hamel, *The Future of Management*, 91-92.

CASE STUDIES: GOOGLE

¹ Google, Life at Google/Why Work at Google?
http://www.google.com/intl/en/jobs/lifeatgoogle/ (accessed on February 1, 2012).

² David Goldman, "Google's Fight to Keep its Top Minds," *CNNMoney*, (November 10, 2010)
http://money.cnn.com/2010/11/10/technology/google_brain_drain/index.htm (accessed on February 1, 2012).

[3] Google, Jobs/Benefits.
http://www.google.com/intl/en/jobs/lifeatgoogle/benefits/
(accessed on February 2, 2012).

[4] Ibid., Benefits Philosophy.

[5] Ibid., Benefits.

[6] Ibid., Company/The Google Culture/About Our Offices.
http://www.google.com/about/company/culture.html (accessed on
February 2, 2012).

[7] Ibid., Company/The Google Culture.

[8] *The Washington Post,* "On Leadership: Google CEO Eric
Schmidt on Workplace Culture," video, 7:27,
http://www.washingtonpost.com/national/on-leadership-google-
ceo-eric-schmidt-on-workplace-
culture/2011/07/15/gIQAajkPGI_video.html (accessed on October
10, 2011).

[9] Michael Burchell and Jennifer Robin, *The Great Workplace*
(San Francisco: Jossey-Bass, 2011), 58.

[10] Nicholas Carlson, "Google CEO Eric Schmidt: We Really
Don't Have a Five-Year Plan," *Business Insider* (May 20, 2009),
http://articles.businessinsider.com/2009-05-
20/tech/30099731_1_google-ceo-eric-schmidt-googlers-google-
people (accessed on February 2, 2012).

[11] *The Washington Post,* "On Leadership: Google CEO Eric
Schmidt on Workplace Culture."

[12] Google, Company/The Google Culture.
http://www.google.com/about/company/culture.html (accessed on
February 2, 2012).

13 Ibid., Company/Our Mission. http://www.google.com/about/company/ (accessed on February 2, 2012).

14 Ibid., Company/Our Philosophy. http://www.google.com/about/company/tenthings.html (accessed on February 2, 2012).

15 Ibid.

16 "Corporate Culture Example: Google's Eric Schmidt on Culture & Hiring," *Corporate Culture Pros* (July 6, 2011), http://www.corporateculturepros.com/2011/07/corporate-culture-example-google-hiring/ (accessed on February 2, 2012).

17 Ibid.

18 "Google: Obsessed with its Employees," *FINS TECHNOLOGY,* (May 11, 2011), http://it-jobs.fins.com/Articles/SB130505696841014767/Google-Obsessed-With-Its-Employees (accessed on February 2, 2012).

19 Ibid.

20 *The Washington Post,* "On Leadership."

21 "Google: Obsessed," *FINS TECHNOLOGY.*

22 Google, Jobs/Hiring Process. http://www.google.com/jobs/joininggoogle/hiringprocess/index.html (accessed on February 2, 20121).

23 Burchell and Robin, *The Great Workplace*, 58.

24 Google, Jobs/Hiring Process.

25 Ibid., Jobs/Top Ten Reasons to Work at Google.

[26] Amy Lyman, "Building Trust by Welcoming Employees," *Great Place to Work Institute,* (2007), 3 http://www.google.com/#sclient=psy-ab&hl=en&source=hp&q=building+trust+by+welcoming+employees&aq=0&aqi=g1g-v3&aql=&oq=&pbx=1&bav=on.2,or.r_gc.r_pw.,cf.osb&fp=782384432d316272&biw=1408&bih=775 (accessed on February 2, 2012).

[27] *The Washington Post,* "On Leadership: Google CEO Eric Schmidt on Workplace Culture."

[28] Ibid.

[29] Roslyn Frenz, "Google's Organizational Structure," *eHow Money,* (2008) http://www.ehow.com/about_6692920_google_s-organizational-structure.html (accessed on February 2, 2012).

CASE STUDIES: SAS

[1] Amy Lyman, "SAS Institute: 2010 #1 Company to Work for in America," *Great Place to Work Institute, Inc.,* (2010), 4 resources.greatplacetowork.com/article/pdf/sas_2010.pdf (accessed on February 3, 2012).

[2]. Laura Schneider, "SAS Institute Company Profile," *About.com Tech Careers,* (2008) http://jobsearchtech.about.com/od/companyprofiles/p/SAS_Institute.htm (accessed on February 2, 2012).

[3] SAS, Company/Corporate Responsibility/Employee/Culture. http://www.sas.com/company/csr/employees.html (accessed on February 3, 2012).

[4] Schneider, "SAS Institute Company Profile."

[5] Justine Costigan, "Benefits, The Hidden Tool of Strategic Growth," *ForbesCustom.com,* (2008)

<u>http://www.forbescustom.com/HCMPgs/HCMBenefitsP1.html</u>
(accessed on February 3, 2012).

⁶ Ibid.

⁷ SAS, Careers/United States/U. S. Employee Benefits and
Programs. <u>http://www.sas.com/jobs/USjobs/benefits.html</u> (accessed
on February 3, 2012).

⁸ Ibid.

⁹ SAS, News/Press Releases/SAS again a top family-friendly
company, leads in benefits and family support (September 8, 2009)
<u>http://www.sas.com/news/preleases/carolinaparentfamily50.html</u>
(accessed on February 3,2012).

¹⁰ Rebecca Leung, "Working The Good Life," *cbsnews.com,*
(February 11, 2009),
1<u>http://www.cbsnews.com/stories/2003/04/18/60minutes/main5</u>
<u>50102.shtml</u> (accessed on February 3, 2012).

¹¹ "SAS Institute CEO Jim Goodnight on Building Strong
Companies—and a More Competitive U. S. Workforce,"
Knowledge@Wharton, (January 5, 2011),3
<u>http://knowledge.wharton.upenn.edu/article.cfm?articleid=2660</u>
(accessed on February 3, 2012).

¹² SAS, News/Press Releases/SAS revenue jumps 2.2% to
record $2.31 billion, (January 21, 2010)
<u>http://www.sas.com/news/preleases/2009financials.html</u> (accessed
on February 3,2012).

¹³ "SAS Institute CEO Jim Goodnight on Building Strong
Companies," *Knowledge@Wharton.*

¹⁴ Leung, "Working The Good Life," 3.

¹⁵ Nigel Barber, "What Makes Workers Happy? Lessons From
the Best Company to Work For," *The Human Beast/Psychology Today,*

(June 1, 2011) http://www.psychologytoday.com/blog/the-human-beast/201106/what-makes-workers-happy-lessons-the-best-company-work (accessed on February 3, 2012).

[16] "100 Best Companies to Work For 2012," *CNNMoney/SAS* (2012) http://money.cnn.com/magazines/fortune/best-companies/2012/snapshots/3.html (accessed on February 3,2012).

[17] SAS, News/Press Releases/SAS Again Ranks No. 1 on FORTUNE Best Companies to Work For in America, (January 20, 2011) http://www.sas.com/news/preleases/2011fortuneranking.html (accessed on February 3, 2012).

[18] Susanne Gargiulo, "How Employee Freedom Delivers Better Business," *CNN.com* (September 21, 2011) http://edition.cnn.com/2011/09/19/business/gargiulo-google-workplace-empowerment/index.html (accessed on February 3, 2012).

[19] Burchell and Robin, *The Great Workplace,* 25.

[20] Mohan Thite, *Managing People in the New Economy* (Thousand Oaks, California, Sage Publications, 2004), 68.

[21] Ibid., 68-69.

[22] Lyman, "SAS Institute: 2010 #1 Company to Work for in America," 4.

[23] SAS, Home. http://www.sas.com/en_us/company-information.html/ (accessed on May 12, 2014).

[24] SAS, Careers/Working at SAS: An Ideal Environment for New Ideas. http://www.sas.com/jobs/corporate/index.html (accessed on February 3, 2012).

25 "SAS Corporate Social Responsibility Summary," 2010. www.sas.com/company/csr/S55232_csr_2010_0603.pdf (accessed on February 3, 20121).

26 SAS, Company/Corporate Responsibility/Education Philanthropy. http://www.sas.com/company/csr/education.html (accessed on February 3, 2012).

27 Ibid., Company/Corporate Responsibility. http://www.sas.com/company/csr/index.html (accessed on February 3, 2012).

28 "SAS Institute: 2010 #1 Company to Work for in America," 3.

29 SAS, Company/Corporate Responsibility/Hiring and Retaining Staff. http://www.sas.com/company/csr_reports/current/employees.html #s1=2 (accessed on February 3, 2012).

30 "SAS Institute: 2010 #1 Company to Work for in America," 3.

31 Annette V. Holesh, HR Program Manager, SAS, "Inspire New Employees with a Strong Onboarding Experience, *Benefits TV* video, 4:20, April 24, 2013, http://ebn.benefitnews.com/video/?id=2732761&page=2.

32 SAS, Company/Corporate Responsibility/Hiring and Retaining Staff.

CASE STUDIES: SOUTHWEST AIRLINES

1 Southwest Corporate Fact Sheet. http://www.swamedia.com/channels/Corporate-Fact-Sheet/pages/corporate-fact-sheet (accessed on May 13, 2014).

2 "Customer Service Champs," *Bloomberg Businessweek*, (March 5, 2007).

http://www.businessweek.com/magazine/content/07_10/b402400
1.htm (accessed on February 3, 2012).

³ Southwest Corporate Fact Sheet.

⁴ Herb Kelleher, "A Culture of Commitment," *Leader to Leader,* (No. 4 Spring 1997), 4.
http://www.google.com/#sclient=psy-
ab&hl=en&source=hp&q=a+culture+of+commitment+by+herb+kelle
her&aq=2lv&aqi=g-
lv4&aql=&oq=&pbx=1&bav=on.2,or.r_gc.r_pw.,cf.osb&fp=782384432
d316272&biw=1408&bih=775 (accessed on February 3, 2012).

⁵ Ibid.

⁶ "Something Special About Southwest Airlines," *CBS News,*(February 11, 2009).
http://www.cbsnews.com/stories/2007/08/30/sunday/main32215
31.shtml (accessed on February 3, 2012).

⁷ "US airline employee incentive plans largely window dressing," *Centre for Asia Pacific Aviation America Airline Daily,* (May 13, 2010). http://www.centreforaviation.com/analysis/us-airline-
employee-incentive-plans-largely-window-dressing-26925 (accessed on February 3, 2012).

⁸ Southwest, Our Benefits.
http://www.southwest.com/html/about-
southwest/careers/benefits.html (accessed on February 3, 2012).

⁹ Kelleher, "A Culture of Commitment," 4.

¹⁰ "Southwest Airlines 2010 One Report: Gary's Message.
http://www.southwestonereport.com/garys-message.php (accessed on February 3, 2012).

¹¹ Kelleher, "A Culture of Commitment," 4.

¹² Ibid., 2.

188   100% Employee Engagement - Guaranteed!

[13] "Southwest Airlines 2010 One Report: Gary's Message/To Our Employees. http://www.southwestonereport.com/mission-vision.php (accessed on February 3, 2012).

[14] Southwest Airlines, About Southwest/Mission. http://www.southwest.com/html/about-southwest/index.html (accessed on February 3, 2012).

[15] Southwest Airlines 2010 One Report: Customers. http://www.southwestonereport.com/people_cu.php (accessed on February 3, 2012).

[16] Southwest Airlines,Fact Sheet/Recognitions. http://www.southwest.com/html/about-southwest/history/fact-sheet.html (accessed on February 3, 2012.

[17] "Ratings and Statistics for Southwest Airlines," *FindTheBest:Airlines*, (2011). http://airlines.findthebest.com/l/22/Southwest-Airlines (accessed on February 3, 2012.

[18] Southwest Airlines, Careers/Our culture. http://www.southwest.com/html/about-southwest/careers/culture.html (accessed on February 4, 2012).

[19] Southwest Airlines, About Southwest. http://www.southwest.com/html/about-southwest/index.html (accessed on February 4, 2012).

[20] Southwest Airlines 2012 One Report: People. http://www.southwestonereport.com/2012/pdfs/2012SouthwestAirlinesOneReport.pdf (accessed on May 13, 2012).

[21] Dawn Gilbertson, "Kelleher Entertains, Enlightens," *The Arizona Republic*, (December 9, 2005), 2. http://www.flyertalk.com/forum/archive/t-502002.html (accessed on February 4, 2012).

[22] Southwest Airlines, Careers/Our People. http://www.swabiz.com/html/about-southwest/careers/our-team.html (accessed on February 4, 2012).

[23] "Southwest Airlines Interview Questions & Reviews," *Glassdoor,* (January 27, 2012), 1-3. http://www.glassdoor.com/Interview/Southwest-Airlines-Interview-Questions-E611.htm (accessed on February 4, 2012).

[24] Cheryl Hughey, "All Aboard: Embarking Employees on the Flight of Their Life," *Human Resources IQ,* (September 10, 2008). http://www.humanresourcesiq.com/talent-management/articles/all-aboard-embarking-employees-on-the-flight-of-th/ (accessed on February 4, 2012).

[25] Ibid.

[26] Gilbertson, "Kelleher Entertains, Enlightens," 1.

[27] Southwest Airlines 2012 One Report: Employee Engagement and Recognition. http://www.southwestonereport.com/2012/pdfs/2012SouthwestAirlinesOneReport.pdf (accessed on May 13, 2014).

CASE STUDIES: ZAPPOS

[1] "100 Best Companies to Work For," *CNNMoney* (2014). http://money.cnn.com/magazines/fortune/best-companies/2014/snapshots/38.html?iid=BC14_fl_list (accessed on May 13, 2014).

[2] Glenn Rifkin, "Zappos Races Ahead," *Korn/Ferry Institute Briefings on Talent and Leadership,* 5. http://kornferrybriefings.com/leadership/zappos_races_ahead.php (accessed on February 4, 2012).

3 "Zappos.com Reviews," *Glassdoor*, (January 24, 2012). http://www.glassdoor.com/Reviews/Zappos-com-Reviews-E19906.htm (accessed on February 4, 2012).

4 Zappos, About Zappos.com/Our Benefits. http://about.zappos.com/jobs/why-work-zappos/our-benefits (accessed on February 4, 2012).

5 "100 Best Companies to Work For," *CNNMoney* (2012). http://money.cnn.com/magazines/fortune/bestcompanies/2011/snapshots/6.html (accessed on February 4, 2012).

6 Wikipedia, Zappos.com/Company Culture and Core Values. http://en.wikipedia.org/wiki/Zappos.com (accessed on February 4, 2012).

7 "Zappos.com Reviews," *Glassdoor.*

8 Zappos.com, Inc., *2010 Culture Book* (available free from Zappos Insights-- http://www.zapposinsights.com/culture-book), 103.

9 Hsieh, *Delivering Happiness*, 192.

10 Ibid., 191.

11 Ibid., 193.

12 Ibid., 196.

13 Zappos, Meet Our Monkeys. http://about.zappos.com/meet-our-monkeys/tony-hsieh-ceo (accessed on May 13, 2014.

14 Hsieh, *Delivering Happiness*, 177.

15 "On a Scale of 1 to 10, How Weird Are You?" *New York Times*, (January 9, 2010).

http://www.nytimes.com/2010/01/10/business/10corner.html?pa gewanted=all (accessed on February 4, 20121).

[16] Zappos, About Zappos.com. http://about.zappos.com/ (accessed on February 4, 2012).

[17] Zappos, About Zappos.com/Zappos Family Core Values. http://about.zappos.com/our-unique-culture/zappos-core-values (accessed on February 4, 2012).

[18] Richards, "At Zappos, Culture Pays," 2.

[19] Hsieh, *Delivering Happiness,* 157.

[20] Zappos Insights, People Pack. http://www.zapposinsights.com/people-pack (accessed on February 4, 2012).

[21] Email on file with the author.

[22] Zappos Insights, People Pack.

[23] Ibid.

[24] Ibid.

[25] Ibid.

[26] Hsieh, *Delivering Happiness,* 153.

[27] Ibid., 177.

[28] Ibid.

[29] Ibid., 150.

[30] Richards, "At Zappos, Culture Pays," 3.

CASE STUDIES: FRANK MYERS AUTO MAXX

[1]frankmyersauto.com, About Tracy Myers. www.winstonsalemusedcars (accessed on May 20, 2014).

[2] Inc.com, Frank Myers Auto Maxx. http://www.inc.com/profile/frank-myers-auto-maxx (accessed on May 20, 2014).

[3] frankmyersauto.com, No Commission Zone. http://www.frankmyersauto.net/non-commissioned-car-sales (accessed on May 21, 2014).

[4] Frank Myers Auto Maxx, "Car Men" - Frank Myers Auto Maxx/Myers Family Documentary, YouTube Video, 26:59, http://www.youtube.com/watch?v=ietWhebVMQY (accessed on May 21, 2014).

[5] Frankmyersauto.com, No Commission Zone.

[6] Conversation with Tracy Myers, owner of Frank Myers Auto Maxx, May 28, 2014.

[7]Frank Myers Auto Maxx, "Car Men" - Frank Myers Auto Maxx/Myers Family Documentary.

[8] Frankmyersauto.com, UF Culture. http://www.frankmyersauto.com/uf-culture (accessed on May 22, 2014).

[9] Ibid.

[10] Frank Ziegler, "Used Car Dealer Invests in Technology Frank Myers Auto Max," *autodealer.com (April, 2007).* http://www.autodealermonthly.com/channel/dps-office/article/story/2007/04/used-car-dealer-invests-in-technology-frank-myers-automaxx.aspx (accessed on May 23, 2014).

[11] Frankmyersauto.com, No Commission Zone.

[12] Conversation with Tracy Myers, Owner of Frank Myers Auto Maxx.

[13] frankmyersauto.com, Join The Team. http://www.frankmyersauto.com/employment (accessed on May 21, 2014).

ABOUT THE AUTHORS

ROSS RECK, PHD

Ross is the coauthor of *Instant Turnaround!*, *REVVED!* and the best selling *The Win-Win Negotiator*. He is also the author of *Turn Your Customers into Your Sales Force*, *The X-Factor* and his very popular newsletter: *Ross Reck's Weekly Reminder*.

A compelling and dynamic speaker, Ross has been featured at hundreds of meetings, conferences and conventions throughout the United States, Canada, Latin America, Europe and Asia. His consulting clients include Hewlett-Packard, John Deere, American Express, Janssen-Ortho, Inc., Shire Pharmaceuticals, Philip Morris International, the Chicago Cubs, Nestle Mexico, Rolls-Royce and Xerox.

Ross received his Ph.D. from Michigan State University in 1977. From 1975 to 1985 he served a Professor of Management at Arizona State University. During his career at ASU he was the only two-time recipient of the prestigious "Teaching Excellence in Continuing Education" award and was identified by the university as an "Outstanding Teacher." Since 1985 he has dedicated his full time efforts to improving the way that the world does business.

TRACY MYERS, CMD

Tracy is an award-winning small business marketing & branding solutions specialist, car dealership owner, best-selling author, Emmy-winning movie producer, speaker, business coach, wrestling promoter and entrepreneur. He is commonly referred to as The Nation's Premier Automotive Solutions Provider while Best-Selling author and legendary speaker Brian Tracy called him "a visionary... a Walt Disney for a new generation."

He is also a Certified Master Dealer and was the youngest ever recipient of the National Quality Dealer of the Year award by the NIADA, which is the highest obtainable honor in the used car industry. His car dealership, Frank Myers Auto Maxx, was recently recognized as the number one Small Business in NC by Business Leader Magazine, one of the Top 3 dealerships to work for in the country by The Dealer Business Journal, one of the Top 15 Independent Automotive Retailers in the United States by Auto Dealer Monthly Magazine and one of the fastest growing privately owned small businesses in America by Inc. magazine.

Tracy has been featured in publications such as Forbes, USA Today and Success Magazine, been profiled on The Biography Channel and The History Channel, written for Fast Company, been a guest business correspondent for the FOX News Network plus he's appeared on NBC, ABC and CBS affiliates across the country. His inspirational stories and strategies for success have given him the opportunity to share the stage with the likes of Jack Canfield, Zig Ziglar (Author of See You At The Top), James Malinchak (Star of ABC's The Secret Millionaire), Brian Tracy, Bob Burg (Co-Author of The Go-Giver), Tom Hopkins and Neil Strauss (Author of The Game

& Co-Author of The Dirt with Motley Crue)... just to name a few.

Tracy is recognized as one of the top thought-leaders in the business world and has authored or co-authored 7 best-selling books alongside Brian Tracy (Author of Eat That Frog), Jack Canfield (Author of The Secret, Creator of the Chicken Soup for the Soul Series), Tom Hopkins (Author of How To Master The Art Of Selling) and many others, including the breakthrough #1 hit YOU Are The Brand, Stupid!. He was also featured in the Emmy nominated film "Car Men", which won 5 Telly Awards, and won 2 Emmy Awards as the Executive Producer of the films "Esperanza" and 'Mi Casa Hogar'.

As the founder and co-moderator of the Unfair Advantage Automotive Mastermind Group, he helps facilitate and stimulate the thought process of some of the auto industry's brightest minds 3 times a year in Charlotte, NC.

As founder of WrestleCade Entertainment, he produces and promotes one of the largest sports entertainment events held annually on the East Coast which has raised thousands for charity and broken attendance records.

Tracy spends his spare time with charities that are close to his heart and has made his home in Lewisville, NC with his wife Lorna and their two children, Presley and Maddie.

THOM SCOTT

A 27-year veteran of advertising and marketing, Thom Scott's passion is to help business owners, C-suite executives as well as authors and speakers build massive and profitable audiences for their products, services and messages.

As a sought-after consultant and corporate executive, Thom has worked in a variety of environments from entrepreneurial to enterprise-level in over 32 different industries. He is often brought in on key initiatives as a "hired gun" by other marketers and agencies.

Having sold his first products online in 1989 via CompuServe classified ads, Thom is a true pioneer in internet marketing. However, his fully integrated marketing approach utilizes the most effective online AND offline tools for each client's unique needs.

Thom has taught his social media and content marketing systems to audiences nationwide and has shared the platform with such notables as Zig Ziglar, Bob Burg, Bob Proctor, Bill Bartmann, Frank McKinney, Les Brown and Stedman Graham.

Contact Information

Ross reck, PhD

To contact Ross regarding his speaking availability, his consulting services, to subscribe to his free weekly newsletter or just to say hello, you are welcome to utilize any of the following options:

Cell phone: 602-391-3250
Web site: www.rossreck.com
Email: ross@rossreck.com
Facebook: Ross Reck
Twitter: @rossreck
LinkedIn: Ross Reck

Tracy Myers, CMD

To contact or communicate with Tracy, please visit:

Website: TracyMyers.com
Facebook: TheTracyMyers
Twitter: @RealTracyMyers
G+: +TracyMyers
Instagram: RealTracyMyers

THOM SCOTT

To contact Thom, please use any of the following options:

Phone: 407-494-3134
Email: <u>legacyarchitect@gmail.com</u>
Facebook: <u>Facebook.com/ThomScott</u>
Twitter: @ThomScott
LinkedIn: <u>LinkedIn.com/in/CoachThom</u>
Instagram: <u>Instagram.com/CoachThom</u>
Google +: <u>https://plus.google.com/+ThomScott/posts</u>
Pinterest: <u>Pinterest.com/ThomScott</u>
Resume: <u>About.me/TheThomScott</u>